Testimonials

What those who are shaping cities say about the book ...

"The book challenges us to rethink urban development, incorporating the powerful perspectives of women into the fabric of our cities. It calls for action, encouraging us to embrace diverse perspectives towards a future where cities work better for women and girls, ultimately benefiting us all."

Ana Paricio Cárceles, Urban Psychologist, Barcelona Regional

"What if Women Designed the City? is an exceptional book, containing tangible and practical ideas to bring about positive change in how women shape and experience public spaces. As an urban planner, I believe the insights in this book could be transformative for those of us in the frontline of delivering this change. A book that is insight-full, tangible and practical whilst, I dare to say, quite emotional."

Daisy Narayanan MBE, Head of Placemaking and Mobility, Edinburgh City Council

"Through the lived experiences of women, this book invites us to imagine urban spaces that benefit everyone. It emphasizes the role of women as active contributors rather than passive subjects, highlighting their transformative role in shaping and revitalising the city. Drawing from diverse real-life examples, this pragmatic book serves as a valuable source of inspiration."

Audrey Hénocque, 1st Deputy Mayor, Responsible for Gender-Sensitive Budget, City of Lyon

"Give women a greater voice in city making and what would you get? A more human centred, emotional satisfying, well balanced, seamlessly connected, safer and probably more beautiful place which thrives on its distinctiveness, values of togetherness and care. So, if women designed the city, that is actually what all of us want, whoever we are. Thank you, May East, for letting us hear those 274 women's voices and their proposed catalytic

interventions and not to forget the marvellous examples interwoven throughout from across the world."

Charles Landry, Author – Creative City: A Toolkit of Urban Innovators

"What if Women Designed the Cities? beautifully presents a sense of hope and power in how we can reset the urban planning gender gap. East's book provides a rich tapestry of leverage points on how cities can regenerate into safe and vibrant communities, allowing everyone to flourish. Politicians, city planners, construction and consultancy firms should read this."

Councillor Holly Bruce, Scottish Green Party, Glasgow City Council

"This is a very timely book, an effective antidote to the soulless, angular, concrete and glass high-rise city that is designed to serve the interests of capital rather than of ordinary people. Will anybody listen? Yes, I think so. Women-inspired urban 'regenerative development' is now an urgent necessity. This is an important book that should be essential reading for anybody concerned about the future of the human habitat."

Herbert Girardet, Author – Creating Regenerative Cities

"The book skilfully guides the reader into the complexity of gender, power and our urban environments. It shows concrete examples that serve as an inspiration while at the same time showcasing how important it is to acknowledge complexity and not least to inform and remind the reader that women are experts of their own space. The book offers guidance and strength to all who want to re-think our urban environments."

Linda Gustafsson, Gender Equality Strategist, City of Umeå

"The book is both moving and inspiring. It positions cities as a vehicle for women's emancipation. Achieving this would undoubtedly be a tremendous accomplishment for Glasgow."

Sarah Shaw, Head of Planning, Glasgow City Council

What if
Women
Designed
the City?

What if Women Designed the City?

33 leverage points to make your city work better for women and girls

May East

Triarchy Press

Published in this first edition in 2024 by:

Triarchy Press
Axminster, UK

www.triarchypress.net

A catalogue record for this book is available from the British Library.

ISBNs:
Print: 978-1-913743-87-1
Ebook: 978-1-913743-88-8

Cover design and illustrations by Sebastian Franke
Cover photo by May East

Triarchy Press

Dedicated to
Athena Polias, Protectress of Ageless Cities

Table of Contents

Foreword One

One would not expect to find a masterful tutorial in regenerative thinking and engagement in a book titled *What if Women Designed the City?* Yet that is exactly what May East delivers. To be clear, the topic of this book is not regenerative development or design. Nor is it a treatise on the problems from and solutions for the longstanding gender gap in urban planning. While the gender gap and its worrisome consequences are mentioned, East makes it clear that her research and the results of the innovative engagement process she designed and tested came from specifically **not** viewing it as a problem to be solved but rather, "as a potential to be unleashed."

"Solving" gender exclusion as a problem could simply mean more women involved in more planning in more places. Flipping the perspective from problem to potential, a core characteristic of regenerative thinking, expands the scope of consideration and reorders what is truly meaningful and significant. East didn't ignore the issue. Instead, she chose to adopt a regenerative lens for her exploration, looking for what ends addressing gender exclusion could serve that would both inspire and require a much higher order of innovation and capability from all involved and reconcile existing divisions. The aim she arrived at — "creating the conditions for cities to transform, evolve and self-organize themselves" served as both end point and North star shaping the design of her innovative research process and the results captured in a "mosaic of visions that could be leveraged by women themselves, co-evolved by residents, urban planners, policy makers, developers, retailers and communities."

The result is a sophisticated multi-dimensional exploration of how the "symbiotic relationships between women and cities" can be developed and supported toward fostering regenerative neighbourhoods. Walking interviews with 274 women explore the roles women can play in city development, and the reciprocal value that can generate for women, their neighbourhoods and ultimately the future life and health of cities and the places they inhabit. The rich tapestry of ideas that emerged are augurs of what women can and do bring to the development of our cities and their future, as well as an indicator of the promise regenerative processes hold.

Shifting our perspective to a regenerative lens (or paradigm), and away from what Carol Sanford calls "do good", changes what we see by changing how we see. Working regeneratively flips the leading question from what we need to *do* to who we need to *become* and what new ableness that will require us to reach for. In consequence it is deeply developmental. It also moves our focus from reparative to generative. As regenerative designers, East notes, women were not very interested in "managing the entropy of failing systems and solving urban problems one at a time."

The last ten years have seen a burgeoning interest in the promise of regenerative development and design. The ability to deliver on that promise however continues to be limited by the gap in understanding of the profound difference between current sustainability practices and regenerative practice and what it requires. The concepts of starting from potential and aiming for goals that generate systemic value have been gaining attention, but they just touch the surface of the fundamental shifts in being and thinking required.

In *What if Women Designed the City?* East fills in this gap, but not in the conventional way of describing what regenerative thinking and engagement are (which would accomplish the opposite). Instead, she invites the reader into experiencing a regenerative process through making explicit her own process – precisely and clearly communicating what shaped it, and what it required her to develop in herself and to enable the development of in those she engaged. This leaves the decision and the onus on the reader to author their own inner work and understanding, another characteristic of regenerative thinking – i.e., that we cannot make the outer transformations required to create a truly sustainable world without making the inner transformations—in ourselves and in those we work with and for.

To create an experiential understanding of a regenerative way of thinking and being, East invites the reader into a journey through a dynamic, multilayered, multidimensional living matrix that requires continually weaving inner and outer worlds. As support, East provides wayfinding guideposts throughout the book. Concepts such as reflexivity, 'presency', co-evolving mutualism and more are presented not as separate ideas but rather as threads that, when woven together, reveal a new order of potential agency and meaning.

The result is a book that requires reflective reading and a conscious choice on the part of the reader in order to realise this value. It is a choice that is implicit in Lorna Kohler's song lyric quoted in the preface: *'I am the weaver. I am the woven one.'* One can take away only what is needed to be the weaver, or one can also step into the process to be the woven one. To be both is to step onto a regenerative path. I am hopeful that more readers will choose the latter for our world's sake.

Pamela Mang
Principal, Regenesis Institute

Foreword Two

As a young planner working for the City of Vienna, I was asked if I wanted to support a planning workshop for a women's politics weekend, organised by the Viennese Social Democratic Women's Organisation, but open to all interested in the topic. Instead of delivering conventional professional planning content rooted in readings about feminist planning demands, I opted to explore the personal experiences of the participating women. We discussed the experience of their housing situations, daily routines, neighbourhood dynamics, mobility, and safety concerns. They encompassed a diverse group, ranging from young planning students to seasoned party members. Through this inter-generational and multidimensional dialogue, we sparked a captivating exchange evolved into continued meetings.

In 1990, our discussions materialised into an exhibition entitled 'Who Needs Public Space? Women's Everyday Life in the City' presented by the Structural Planning Department of the City. Drawing 4,000 visitors and capturing extensive media attention, this signified a ground-breaking moment – women advocating for their role in shaping urban structures – and marked the inception of institutionalised gender planning policies in Vienna, even before the term existed. At the time, mainstream traffic planners largely overlooked pedestrian needs and rarely considered walking a key mode of transportation. The value of parks, squares and playgrounds as social capital for the neighbourhood was not realised. We, however, championed user-centric perspectives, emphasising daily travel patterns, caregiving responsibilities, also children's, teens and elderly people's needs.

Our pioneering work led to studies, pilot projects and full-scale implementations across critical domains such as housing subsidies, park design, public spaces, safety measures, mobility, and urban design. Vienna's transformation attracted interest from other cities seeking to implement a female perspective in urban development, positioning Vienna as a source of inspiration in this realm. Perhaps this is why May East extended an invitation to me to write the foreword for this book. As I immersed myself in its concepts and leverage points, I felt a resurgence of that thrilling energetic feeling from Vienna's early days.

The language employed here isn't cloaked in technocratic or academic jargon; it is close to everyday speech – clear and concise, yet never oversimplified. The approach, rooted in walks and conversations, centres on everyday knowledge within neighbourhoods. These low-barrier, inclusive methods also provide room to learn about demands, desires and visions. Trusting the expertise of participating women in their daily lives, caregiving responsibilities, bodily experiences, and emotions contrasts with the mainstream planner's presumption of knowing what's best for all, often stemming from a male perspective.

For me, tangible examples are more convincing than the most brilliant theoretical concepts. Real stories encourage, as they reveal potential. If something has been accomplished somewhere, it can take place elsewhere. This book includes a collection of these storylines, forming the blueprint of a city envisaged by women, a vision brought to life.

This book goes far beyond conventional gender planning as an institutionalised strategy. It is holistic and focuses on potentials, not on challenges, deficits and problems. This shift in perspective is inspiring, essential for triggering the transformations our cities need, especially amidst climate crises.

The vision of a car-free cityscape, evoking a Venetian ambiance with bike lanes and pedestrian zones replacing canals, is compelling. The reduction of car traffic to essential and emergency needs is imperative. A vast majority of streets could transform into lush green oases and communal spaces – especially in urban heat island zones often occupied by the most socioeconomically disadvantaged. Women, who historically have been caregivers, tend to embrace necessary changes, envisioning positive outcomes, and then rallying support for the cause.

May East's book also brilliantly showcases women's potential as both advocates and activists, offering inspiration not only to women but also to politicians. In the face of the pressing climate crisis, the need for structural changes is apparent. However, politicians, though well-aware of the necessary changes, require our pressure and the support of citizens who see the gains and not the threats in changing mobility habits and land use.

Had the feminist perspectives introduced since the 1970s gained mainstream traction, our cities of today would be more climate resilient. Our urgent focus should now be on managing the imperative changes, utilising the limited time available to us to confront the climate crisis. Just as male engineers reshaped urban systems in the late 19th century through technical innovations, today's transformation requires a comparably radical approach with active female involvement.

Socially sustainable, post-fossil fuel urban redevelopment is a big chance! We should swiftly adopt a systemic perspective, positioning caregiving at its core. This book is informative, inspiring and encouraging, published just at the right moment as windows of opportunities are fast closing – we must ensure they remain open with all our might. This book can help us do so!

Eva Kail
Senior Planner and Gender Planning Expert, City of Vienna

Preface

Most of my life I have lived, worked and felt at home in vibrant cities such as São Paulo, New York, London, Amsterdam, Paris, and Edinburgh. Blending in with the crowd, cities influenced my identity and even my name – May East Side (of Manhattan). Early on my journey, I learned the truth of *solvitur ambulando*, sorting things in my mind while strolling through streets, *avenidas* and alleyways. Immersed in a multitude of inter-actions with strangers, cities taught me when to stand-up and when to escape the gaze. For me nothing heals a wounded heart more than a vigorous walk through the city. Nothing excites me more than 'taking a walk on the wild side', full of presence even if there is no one there.

I have experienced cities as places of discovery, meaning-making, disruption and transformation. I have witnessed cities grow and become innovative, as well as dysfunctional, blurring the boundaries between the natural and built environments, or becoming a wasteland of billboards fuelling unnecessary consumerism.

For 14 years, I lived and learned in a most thrilling laboratory for urban settlement design: the Findhorn Ecovillage in Scotland. And from there, I established a UN Training Centre for Local Authorities conducting capacity development activities under the thematic area of urban design for carbon-constrained settlements and lifestyles. For a period, I joined the Transition Towns movement, and as a transition trainer I seeded its simple place-based principles and methodologies as wide as Vila Brasilândia, the largest slum settlement in Brazil and South America more broadly, as well as in villages under the leadership of the Federation of Tribal Women of Kakariguma, in the Indian state of Odisha. Today I work with mining cities, striving to diversify their economic flows in a regenerative manner and establishing sovereign wealth funds to avert financial and ecological debts being passed on to future generations.

Bridging the gap between theory and practice, my Master's study focused on how to regenerate a growing stock of abandoned ghost towns in Southern Italy. Fast forward, when the time came for a PhD, I looked at the continuities and discontinuities of the city and pondered... what are the regenerative frameworks enabling cities that work for women and girls? This led me to the concept of the historical urban planning gender gap and the question: What if Women Designed the City? Exploring this line of enquiry became the focus of my study and the topic of this book.

A word of caution. In academic research, gender influences who pursues the research, how and which research questions are identified as important. It also informs which methodologies are chosen, the case studies and data sets used, and the analysis undertaken. In the spirit of self-reflexivity, I acknowledge my standpoint as a white able-bodied cisgender educated woman born in the Global South, and whose professional growth has taken place in the Global North in the context of international institutions.

I have been a practitioner for most of my professional life. In the process of 'becoming' a researcher I have drawn from the lessons of Paulo Freire, who proposed the notion of 'conscientisation' ('conscientização' in Portuguese), which refers to the process of developing 'critical consciousness' of one's social reality through reflection and action. In this context, I cultivated three 'awarenesses' throughout my fieldwork while walking with 274 women, viewed as experts of their neighbourhoods in the Scottish cities of Glasgow, Edinburgh and Perth.

The first awareness relates to the story of appropriation. In the attempt to be inclusive and conceptualise difference and diversity, I am aware of the unfairness that is compounded in the 'appropriation' of the voices of 'others'. As a woman originally from the Global South, it feels effortless to establish rapport with women from the same hemisphere. However, I made considerable effort not to reinforce patterns of cultural appropriation or even 'maternalism', in my 'privileged' role as researcher, even if temporarily, when incorporating the voices of those who are often absent in urban planning discussions.

Reflexivity in this context, meant thinking critically about my Southern presence and energy 'signature', sometimes embodied as unbounded enthusiasm! By being reflexive, I attempted to co-develop reciprocal alliances based on empathy and mutual respect, but also to provide space for women participants to withdraw comfortably at any stage of the conversation. Adopting walking interviews where women had control over the research process, deciding at what time they wished to start and finish interviews and where to go, provided flexibility and encouraged sensitivity to the power relations informing participant-researcher dynamics.

The second awareness centred around sensitivity in the creation of conditions for women to engage in generative thinking in the open air. As researcher, I brought my urban experiences and background to my fieldwork, which meant reigning in any temptation to supply participants with my thoughts instead of creating conditions for women to generate their own unique insights and conceptualisations. This process required me to be self-observant, open to diverse mindsets and genuinely curious about the thought processes of the women I walked with.

The third awareness, related to a shift in my focus from concentrating on problems to potentials. Over the decades, I have nourished a sustained interest in the role of women in designing an inclusive and calculated revolution in the way we plan, walk, live, interact with family, do business, and pursue recreation in our cities, to counteract the 'zoned' city concept in which housing, work, commerce and recreation are segregated into separate locations. I believe that women themselves remain best suited to elucidate their position within society and the city. I therefore acknowledge my sensitivities and life experience proved to be important tools in helping me to make sense of the perspectives of the women I engaged with in my research.

Thus, I did not view the gender gap in urban planning as a problem to be solved but rather a potential to be realised. Acknowledging that women can contribute to urban planning decisions and implementation, and in doing so enrich and add value to urban environments and more specifically to their own neighbourhoods, is a core assumption that this book builds upon. Holding a perspective which emphasises potential rather than problems during my walking interviews occasionally surprised the women I engaged, who were primed towards making a list of problems for which responsibility lay elsewhere.

While diversity of perspectives was valued, employing a reflexive approach to my fieldwork allowed me to be open to contrasting opinions, particularly those that might contradict my own, helping me avoid getting boxed into only finding 'strongs' in the system rather than 'wrongs'. In short, by practising empathetic consideration and attempting to perceive the city through the eyes of the women I spoke with, I was able to expand my thought horizons and savour the unexpected beauty of their everyday experiences.

This book weaves insights from my fieldwork in Scotland with my evolving social-spatial observations from visiting, walking and transforming myself in the process of exploring and deciphering cities: New York, Vienna, Barcelona, Santa Cruz, Lille, Glastonbury, Florianópolis, Copenhagen, Alicante, Lisbon, Istanbul, amongst others. These cities are made of thousands of villages and neighbourhoods. Moving from bustling city centres to deserted post-industrial territories populated by warehouses and vacant lots; from tightly knit communities to modernist areas characterised by absence of soul, I frequently recall the lyrics from Lorna Kohler's song: *'I am the weaver (of the urban fabric). I am the woven one'*.

I dedicate my efforts to the spirit of my late mother, Helena, and to her generation of women who witnessed rapid changes in their urban environments – sometimes limiting and sometimes widening the experience of being a woman in a city.

Lastly, my work draws on generations of women cited in this book, many of whom worked in the urban planning field long before I entered it. I am grateful for and to them.

May East
Shakespeare & Co
New York
20 April 2023

1 | The Context

'It is easy to accept the physical landscape
unthinkingly as a neutral background.'
~ Leslie Kanes Weisman ~

Women architects, urban geographers and planners have, over the years, been integral to exploring cities and the role that women play in shaping and being shaped by them. While there has been research on how urban planning fails to respond to women's needs and perspectives, the concept of an 'urban planning gender gap' remains under-theorised and under-represented in the realm of practical applications. [1] [2] [3] [4]

This book emerges at the intersection between two megatrends informing the world we live in: women's repositioning in society and the accelerated pace of urbanisation. It builds upon a series of recent documents and reports by international 'agenda holders' [5] [6] and 'knowledge brokers' [7] [8] [9] reaffirming that, historically, cities have been planned and built primarily through taking the male experience as the reference. As a result, cities tend to function better for men than they do for women.

The systematic exclusion of women from urban planning means women's daily lives and perspectives rarely shape urban form and function. [10] Furthermore, what is known as gender-neutrality in urban planning is nothing of the sort: it usually adopts a male perspective, reproducing gender stereotypes and often limiting women's realities to the role and function of carer.[11]

In this book, a woman is defined as a person who identifies as female within the spectrum of current discourses around gender identity. I have been asked on several occasions about how cities designed by women may differ from cities designed by men. A comparative study between genders was certainly not the focus of my thesis research. Future research could certainly engage in similar enquiry, as well as from the perspective of other gender identities and indeed other identified demographic, social and cultural communities.

I am convinced that the future of humanity and the biosphere will be decided by the way we choose to evolve our cities and towns in the 21st Century. Cities cover a mere 4% of the planet surface[12] but account for 80% of global energy consumption,[13] 75% of carbon emissions [14] and more than 75% of the world's natural resources.[15] 4.2 billion people now live in cities and towns, and 3 billion more are expected to do so within 40 years.[16]

Cities also generate their own wealth, shape national politics and are spearheading a thrilling new vision of governance for the coming century. In this context, some would say that in this century, it will be the city – not the state – that becomes the nexus of economic and political power. Indeed, in many cases city officials are responding to transnational problems more effectively than nation-states, caught up as they are in geo-political rivalries.

The case for cities adopting a beyond-sustainability regenerative approach is profoundly compelling. Pragmatic in its orientation, close to people and their problems, cities also contain the seeds of their own regeneration. However, cities have been planned, developed and built primarily by men embedding unequal bio-cultural-spatial patterns in the fabric of urban environments.

Urbanisation is often associated with greater independence and opportunity for women. However, it is also characterised by housing inequality, a transport infrastructure informed by private car ownership, intersectional violence, inadequate disaster preparedness, and decision making that reflects deep gender-based inequalities. Understanding the key urbanisation trends likely to unfold over the coming years, and revisiting the role women may play in their mediation of space and making of place, are crucial to forging a timely gender-sensitive framework of urban development.

This book takes a unique approach to city development by using a living-systems metabolic framework[17] with the goal of creating conditions for cities to evolve, transform and self-organise themselves through circular processes. The book also embraces a gendered perspective of systems thinking for systems change, by asking women to reveal the potential rooted in the uniqueness of their areas and identify leverage points for shifting from 'what is' to 'what if'. I draw on thinking emerging from a regenerative perspective, where cities are viewed as complex living systems in a co-evolving partnership between bio-physical and social-cultural systems, which hold the potential to strengthen social and natural capital rather than deplete them.[18] Core elements of this approach are systems thinking, respect for place, and stakeholder engagement.[19]

At its core, 'design' is understood as an envisioning process conducted as a social practice – as proposed by author Sylvia Margolin and design historian Victor Margolin – implying that urban form is conceived, discussed, and planned, before it is developed.[20] Thus, women as designers are understood as meaning-makers, influencers and shapers of urban form that serves multiple segments of society. Furthermore, design as a process is associated with the capacity to unleash the potential of each unique place (rather than identifying problems to solve) and serves to demonstrate how urban systems can co-evolve with ecological systems.[21] [22]

Place, much like nature, is in constant remaking and transformation. Place here is defined as the unique, multi-layered network of living systems within an urban area, that emerges from the complex interactions between the ecological, socio-cultural, and the built environment systems. I refer to this dynamic interaction as the ever-evolving bio-cultural-spatial uniqueness of place. My hypothesis is that by adopting a bio-cultural-spatial uniqueness of place perspective, urban planners, practitioners and communities can uncover inter-dependent relations between seemingly isolated things, and in turn create more coherent diagnoses, policies, plans, and ultimately performing projects.

Jane Jacobs proposed that wholesale city plans never stirred women's blood,[23] while De Beauvoir claimed that men cannot adequately represent women's interests.[24] While planning was once the near-exclusive realm of specialised male experts, and in the 1990s communicative and collaborative methods became a prerequisite for planning processes,[25] during the 2020s women are stepping up as protagonists in shaping their urban environments. In doing so, many are aiming to value their sense of place, care for their green and blue spaces, engage with an active travel world, and above all explore how cities of both the present and the future can be greener, wilder, more inclusive, liveable, and poetic.

2 | Women and Cities: A Co-Evolving Mutualism Perspective

'If time is the dimension of change, then space is the dimension of coexisting difference.'

~ Doreen Massey ~

There are two predominant perspectives informing 'urban planning gender gap' debates which are concerned with the unique relationship between women and cities. They can be categorised as *urban determinism* (cities constraining and shaping women's experience of the city) and *social determinism* (women affecting the opportunities cities provide), revealing a divide in worldviews, policymaking, and in the physical manifestation of urban environments.

The urban determinism perspective focuses on how cities constrain, disadvantage and oppress women.[26] [27] [28] This line of argument views urban space as fundamentally constructed by gender difference where women are both deprived and excluded from urban planning decisions – which becomes the prerogative of an exclusive segment of society, namely white, middle-aged, able-bodied Western men.[29] Women, in this context, are often 'the planned ones', victimised through urban design choices that shape social arrangements and, as result, influence the experiences of their lives.[30]

Those who criticise the architectural deterministic perspective emphasise the professional arrogance of planners and architects who introduce gendered symbolism into the urban built environment through masculinised forms, including skyscraper seduction.[31] Referring to the office tower, the American poet and professor of architecture Dolores Hayden wrote: '[it] is one more addition to the procession of phallic monuments in history – including poles, obelisks, spires, columns and watch-towers'.[32] The urban deterministic line of argument views women's role in the regeneration of cities as practically challenging. [33] [34]

> The UN Agenda 2030 positions women and girls as diverse and innovative agents of change, and gender equality as central to the achievement of all the Sustainable Development Goals (SDGs). In principle, the narrative seems coherent: cities provide opportunities for women's emancipation, whilst women gain space through urbanisation. While investigating SDG 11 – Sustainable Cities and Communities – at the target level (targets 11.2 and 11.7), the framing of the discourse is revealing. Women are characterised as amongst the vulnerable members of society requiring protection alongside children, older people and persons with disabilities. It is notable that even 40 years after the Convention on the Elimination of all Forms of Discrimination against Women,[35] the international community still associates women with those in need of protection, instead of proposing a political accord that inspires and propels women as subjects of contemporary cities.

By contrast, the social determinism perspective focuses on how cities liberate women, through widening their social-economic horizons and providing them with an escape from normative behaviours – which closely conforms to my own experience growing up in the megacity São Paulo. This way of looking at the relationship between women and cities concerns deconstructing the patriarchy embedded in urban form and function. It embodies a feminist-rights-to-the-city approach. Cities here are understood as ambiguous spaces which can be appropriated by women seeking autonomy and independence.[36] [37] [38] The appealing social mesh of cities provides a 'living landscape' where women can break away from obsolete roles, experience new freedoms, challenge existing stereotypes and shape appropriate policies which take into consideration women's rights to the city. The social determinism body of feminist research argues that space is not the exclusive territory of architecture, and rather envisages context-specific emancipatory possibilities which can transform oppressive models of structural power into territories of appropriation by women.

In her seminal book *Sphinx in the City*, independent researcher Elisabeth Wilson advocates for the social determinism perspective, suggesting that amid the 'urban-ness' of urban life the pattern of women experiencing the city and men designing it can be challenged.[39] Additionally, this perspective asserts that it is within the core of everyday life that we can revisit and challenge the critical connection between power and place. Furthermore, it is at the heart of the lively city which promises a multitude of possibilities, that the dynamics of the *genderfication** of placemaking can be tested,[40] as well as where the re-negotiation of systems of empowerment versus oppression and exclusion, can take place.[41] Reinforcing this view, Wilson claims that cities have provided unprecedented freedoms for women who can benefit from the anonymity and spontaneity made possible within urban environments.[42]

---

* The process where gender-related factors and considerations are intentionally incorporated into urban planning to promote gender equality and address the specific needs and experiences of different genders within a given space or community.

Since the predominant debates discussed above are framed by a dualist paradigm, with two contrasting, mutually exclusive realities, I intentionally sought to redress the balance by proposing an integrated perspective which includes and transcends this analytical divide. Therefore, I suggest a third emerging perspective which is termed *co-evolving mutualism*[*]. Here, women and cities are systemically implicated in the construction of each other in a continuous process of self-organisation and reorganisation, increasing in complexity, definition and information exchange. This perspective acknowledges that contemporary cities can both limit and empower women, who in turn can contribute to a complex network of urban relationships and interventions.

Addressing the question of 'what kind of problem a city is', urbanist and activist, Jane Jacobs, whose writings championed a community-based approach to city building, put forward that cities are essentially problems in organised complexity with many variables interrelated into an organic whole:

> *Cities, like the life sciences, do not exhibit one problem in organised complexity, which if understood explains all. They can be analysed into many such problems or segments which as in the case of the life sciences, are also related with one another. The variables are many, but they are not helter-skelter; they are interrelated into an organic whole.*[43]

The discussion of how cities influence women and how women shape cities is at the heart of this book. The co-evolving mutualism perspective provides the framework by which women and cities can be engaged in an interdependent and mutually beneficial relationship, towards an enriching expression of gender-sensitive cities of today and tomorrow. For this to happen, I view the relationship between women and the

---

[*] A symbiotic relationship where two or more species evolve together, benefiting each other in a mutually advantageous way.

city as a single unbroken movement, generating life-affirming interactions and supported by new patterns of thought and language. Furthermore, by adopting a co-evolving mutualism systems perspective, the pitfalls associated with adopting a zero-sum game[*] perspective, where women's gains are inevitably other people's (men's) loss, are uprooted from the ground up.

Urban planning gender gap existing lines of argument			
Basis of Comparison	Urban Determinism	Social Determinism	Co-evolving Mutualism
Power Relations	Spatially mediated society Spatial fetishism Male-dominated urban environments	Socially produced space Challenges Phallogocentrism[44] Appropriations and Possibilities	Society and space are integral to one another Women and cities are systemically implicated in the construction of each other
Position of Women	Vulnerability Subordination	Confrontational Emancipation	Synergistic Systems Actualisation
Spatial Patterns	Constraining and Restricting Determining	Passively reflecting social relations Providing escape from normative expectations	Dialectical causation Enabling

Table 1: Urban planning gender gap lines of argument

---

[*] A situation where one person's gain is directly balanced by another person's loss.

2.1 Key-Concept – Presency

'The moment you realise you are not present, you are present.'
Eckhart Tolle

Humans exist in language.[45] It is in the spirit of *languaging**
that I introduce a new concept termed 'presency', as a pathway
for involving women and cities in processes of co-evolving
mutualism. The concept blends the words presence and agency,
combining both meanings. It adopts the concept of presence as
a mindful way of paying attention to life, moment by moment,
combined with agency, understood as critical awareness of the
context and capacity to act.

For Paulo Freire,[46] reflection and action are symbiotic elements
that support the development of a critical awareness of one's
social reality. Symbiosis here is understood as the interaction
between two different living systems in close physical
association, typically to the advantage of both.[47] The emphasis
on reflection over action leads to rhetorical verbalism, while
action alone can only bear the fruits of shallow activism and
limited positive change. It is not enough for women to come
together in dialogue to gain knowledge of their urban reality.
Critical reflection uncovering real predicaments improves their
capacity to act intentionally and responsibly to transform their
reality. Thus, the concept of agency adopted here is anchored in
reflection on the present condition of the neighbourhoods in
which women live, propelling them to co-develop purposeful
new lines of work in their urban contexts.

By introducing the concept of 'presency', I acknowledge that
profound changes in the urban environment, such as those
aspired to by contemporary women, seldom emerge from

---

* A process of making meaning and building knowledge through language

'unrepresentative' policy-making processes, nor from purely functional changes to urban infrastructure.

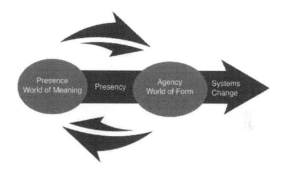

Figure 1: Presency, the self-reinforcing system of reflection and action towards systems change

Transformative change springs from the dynamics between reflection and action, presence and agency, the realm of being and the world of function (also from disruptive and unexpected events). Within this perspective, women are understood as thoughtful actors who may transform themselves in the process of changing their environments.

3 | Systems Thinking for Urban Systems Change

'The crises we face are systemic in nature. To overcome those crises, we need to understand how systems work. To arrive at such an understanding, we need to think systemically.'
~ Ludwig Von Bertalanffy ~

This book is about the symbiotic relationships between women and cities towards fostering regenerative neighbourhoods. Not all symbiotic relationships, however, are regenerative. Therefore, I draw on the concept of regenerative design – as defined by Regenesis Group[48] – to help orientate the symbiotic processes identified in this book towards harmonising human actions with the continuing evolution of life on Earth. This means nurturing conditions for urban communities to re-enter into life-giving alignment with the natural living systems that support them.

Einstein suggested that the mindset that creates a problem in the first place, will not in turn solve it.[49] The intersecting nature of the biophysical, social and economic crises that plague our modern(ist) world, highlights the increasing need for collaboration across diverse disciplines and demands new modes of thinking to understand how the problems we confront are interconnected. Thus, the combined advances in social theory, complexity science and the field of living systems, and social cybernetics[50] has helped to awaken the world from what William Blake called 'Newton's sleep'.[51]

For the historian and philosopher of science, Thomas Kuhn, paradigms and practices that define a scientific discipline change when existing solutions no longer work and emerging issues require new approaches.[52] Responding to the increased complexity of our understanding of the world and the ways in which we attempt to control it, since the 1950s a remarkable diversity of frameworks and methodologies has been birthed from systems thinking.[53] [54]

But what is a system? Inspired by one of the most cited system thinkers of the 1990s, Donella Meadows, I understand a system to be a set of elements, sub-elements or parts interconnected in such a way that they jointly serve an overarching purpose.[55] Systems thinking is therefore the underlying framework for seeing, naming and describing the relationship between these interconnections. When this happens, we can access what writer and educator, Nora Bateson, calls 'warm data',[56] or other types of information and new patterns of connection between elements that, when identified, can unleash new lines of systemic work.

Systems thinking engages complexity, it doesn't pretend it is not there. Thus, systems thinking offers an effective language that help us discuss dynamic complexities and interdependencies, such as those encountered in the multifaceted realities of urban planning and the convergence of place-based possibilities with which planners are involved.

The system we employ to shape our cities is still influenced by the command-and-control thinking of post-war reconstruction and regulatory approaches to the built environment.[57] Urban professionals and politicians (roles historically dominated by men) have traditionally believed that they can control the complex nature of cities through zoning and land use planning, aiming to create functional real estate markets. Many of the decisions are taken behind closed doors. But systems can evolve and diversify.

As you read through this book, I invite you to join me in exploring ways to bridge the historic gender gap in planning through a systemic exploration of the domain and emerging new directions. By centring the able-bodied, working male as the 'neutral' user of the city, modern planning has created urban spaces more suited for men - and often those white, healthy and wealthy – than for women, girls, people with disabilities, and sexual, gender and ethnic minorities. Embedded in the richness of women's everyday life experiences of walking and living in the city, it is hoped that this work reveals unrecorded system interdependencies, widens the spectrum of planning participation and instigates new lines of work which together hold the power to change urban realities.

4 | Leverage Points: Places to Intervene in a System

'A system is a way of looking at the world.'
~ Gerald M. Weinberg ~

Frameworks possess structuring power, and in systems thinking can help us grow our understanding of the complex social, natural and spatial living systems we work and live within. An influential example of such a framework was developed by Donella Meadows. In her essay *'Leverage Points: Places to Intervene in a System'*,[58] Meadows hypothesised that there 'are places within a complex system - which could be a corporation, an economy, a living body, a city, an ecosystem - where a small shift in one thing can produce big changes in everything'.[59] Meadows proposed two types of leverage points: 'shallow' leverage points where a small amount of change force causes a small change in system behaviour; and a 'deep' leverage point where a small amount of change force effects a large change, potentially resulting in transformational change in system behaviour.

Greek mathematician and inventor Archimedes is widely credited with introducing the concept of leverage over 2000 years ago. He stated:

Give me a lever long enough and a fulcrum on which to place it, and I shall move the world.[60]

A lever allows you to concentrate the effort to lift or move objects on a particular inflection point. In this process, where you apply the lever is almost as important as how long the lever is. Similarly, a leverage point is where a small, fine-tuned stimulation in a specific place can lead to significant, enduring improvements in the system as a whole. Like acupuncture points, leverage points are places where a strategic intervention can create lasting change – positive or negative ripple effects that spread far and wide.

Inventor, Richard Buckminster Fuller, utilised the concept of 'trim tab' to refer to leverage points, highlighting that anyone can act as a trim tab.[61] A trim tab is a small rudder located on a larger rudder of a ship or airplane. Its function is to make it easier to turn the larger rudder, which then makes it easier to turn the ship or the plane. He suggested that if a tiny sliver of metal can alter the course of a great ship, any individual can change the course of humanity.

However, Donella Meadows advised us to 'stay humble, stay a learner',[62] before considering intervening into a system. We need to analyse the system standards, structures, rules, and paradigms to discern where it is best to activate and nudge a leverage point within a system towards creating generative, new courses of action. To effect the change we are seeking, we may need to let go of prior assumptions and beliefs concerning how the world works.

She described twelve places to intervene in a system in ascending order of effectiveness, and grouped them into four main analytical categories: Parameters, Feedback Loops, System Structure, and Mental Models.

Leverage Points

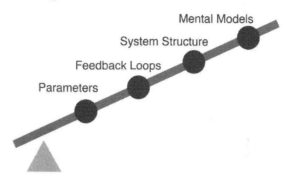

Figure 2: The four categories of leverage points by Donella Meadows

Parameters are numbers described in a system such as taxes, incentives and standards – which might be air quality standards, the amount of land set aside for conservation or the volume of rainfall. This category also includes material interventions such as physical infrastructure, or transport and logistics networks. Meadows positions parameters of least influence in her list of interventions. Although these might be the most visible and recognised among all leverage types, they are usually the slowest and most expensive to effect change in the system, and rarely change behaviours.

Feedback Loops encompass positive and negative conduits of timely and relevant information within a system. While negative feedback loops are self-correcting, positive feedbacks are self-reinforcing. Feedback loops, as an overall category, associates delays in feedback with the pace of change of a system: for example, delays between the identified need for infrastructural change, compared to the length of time necessary for implementation. For Meadows, missing feedback is a significant factor that often leads to system malfunctions.

 The third category – **System Structure** – relates to redefining the rules of the system and information flows through design. It highlights the power of information reaching new previously untapped places in a system, potentially leading to changes in people's behaviour. It also emphasises the power of rules, and equally, who controls them. The ability to add, change, evolve or self-organise a system's structure, highlights the potential of a system to reinvent itself under different conditions.

 Finally, the category **Mental Models** concerns intentionally changing mindsets and paradigms, and reinforces the need to remain flexible and avoid being overly zealous about our own worldviews. It also focuses on who has the power to change the goals of a system, such as challenging the contemporary assumption that 'growth is good' through asking 'who is it good for and who isn't it good for?'

Table 2 overleaf presents Donella Meadows' 12 places to intervene in a system under these 4 main categories.

Categories	Places to intervene in a system (in increasing order of effectiveness)
Parameters	12. Parameters (such as numbers, taxes, standards)
	11. The size of buffer stocks and their flows
	10. The structure of material stocks and flows
Feedback Loops	9. The length of delays, relative to the rate of system change
	8. The strength of negative feedback loops
	7. The gain of driving positive feedback loops
System Structure	6. The structure of information flows (who does and does not have access to what kind of information)
	5. The rules of the system (such as incentives, punishments and constraints)
	4. The power to add, change, evolve or self-organise system structure
Mental Models	3. The goals of the system
	2. The mindset/paradigm out of which the system arises
	1. The power to transcend paradigms

Table 2: The 12 leverage points grouped in four system characteristics [63]

Within her prolific body of thinking, Donella Meadows offered words of caution:

> We can't impose our will upon a system. We can listen to what the system tells us and discover how its properties and our values can work together to bring forth something much better than could ever be produced by our will alone.[64]

I draw on Meadows' leverage points framework to organise the ideas of the women I spoke with and to help visualise, communicate, and share recommendations with local authorities, urban practitioners, and communities on how to design and develop cities with women in mind. The leverage points lens is ideal for framing the findings of walking interviews, encompassing aspects from the very pragmatic (such as how cities could look if pavements were built, public transport networked, alleyways illuminated, and neighbourhood funds distributed), through drawing deeply on the 'presency' of women. It also recognises the influence that the distribution of power, mindset, and rules of the system have in democratising the way women and girls use and experience public space.

5 | Regenerative Design: Bringing Vitality to Urban Systems

'Love of place unleashes the personal and political will needed to make profound change. It can also unite people across diverse ideological spectra because place is what we all share: it is the commons that allows people to call themselves a community.'

~ Pamela Mang ~

Urban regeneration as an applied concept has evolved over time. It has its roots in the functional framework defined by the Athens Charter, which laid the foundations of modern planning.[65] [66] The Charter, supposedly produced by the historic *Congrès Internationaux d'Architecture Moderne* (CIAM) held on board the SS Patris en route from Marseille to Athens in 1933, is regarded as a critical watershed. It marked a new direction for the organically developed urban conglomeration to transform into 'an organised, flawlessly hygienic and structurally transparent urban machine'.[67] This modernist manifesto had a profound influence on the architecture, planning practices and reconstruction of post-war Europe. It advocated for a functional and methodical land policy, with a mechanical separation of living, working, mobility, and leisure activities;[68] and large-scale, technologically rational plans[69] over pre-existent aestheticism and the chaotic division of streets, shops, and houses.

At the dawn of the modernist era, European cities were largely designed and planned by civil engineers, architects, and public health experts – fields dominated by men[70] using a 'universal' aesthetic to build for 'man'; and not necessarily for all men equally either, since class also intersected.[71] Most Western cities bear this imprint of modernist, patriarchal planning.[72] The Athens Charter remains one of the most controversial trends in urban planning and still informs the core planning techniques adopted in zoning approaches, even if applied more flexibly at times. This has had a lasting effect on the lives of contemporary women, particularly those residents of housing schemes.

Planning has always operated under the assumption of a dominant culture. For over a century, 'regeneration' theory and practice has shaped and shifted urban environments (many times targeting 'social exclusion'), responding to changes in living conditions guided by the economic and political forces of the day. At the threshold of the 21st century, an inspiring cadre of regenerative theorists and practitioners attempted to re-position 'regeneration' as a knowledge-based paradigm, grounded in the science of living systems, and on an awareness that every life form is unique and nested within other, larger living systems.[73] [74] [75]

Advocates of regenerative design and development argue that in an unpredictable world, we can help the places where we live and work to thrive, going well beyond merely sustaining a precarious balance between the larger community of life and human essential needs for survival and quality of life.[76] In practice, the concept of regenerative urban development ensures that cities not only become zero-waste and low carbon-emitting but go beyond that by enhancing the relationship between an urbanising humanity and ecosystems which sustain lifestyles.[77] For this collective of 'regeneratists', the design challenge facing urban decision makers is to improve and bring new life to the degraded conditions of soils, green spaces, watercourses and hinterlands. It also means adopting a place-centred approach to counteract the trend of master plans and scale-ability where a particular approach is rolled out around the city with minimal regard to the uniqueness of place.[78]

5.1 A Regenerative Framework of Inquiry

A core insight of regenerative development theory is the idea that we can shift from dominance to intimacy in our relationship with the entity of place.[79] In order to capture women's underlying relationships to the cities they lived in, I developed a six-stage regenerative framework that was capable of being used in diverse contexts and thematic areas to provide a coherent structure to orientate my investigation. As such, this enquiry cycle (Figure 3) was applied equally in each of the four areas I investigated: namely, sense of place, green spaces, active travel, and safety.

Figure 3: The six-stage regenerative framework of enquiry

Stage 1 – Uniqueness of Place

The narrative around the uniqueness of place served as the starting point for my enquiry. By addressing the question 'What is unique about this place?', women were invited to reveal the essential character of a place they were connected to, why people cared about it, and why they need to work together to realise a thriving future. Regenerative theory highlights the symbiotic relationship between place and (at least) two levels of nested systems, sometimes referred to as proximate whole and greater whole (for example a forest, nested in a valley, nested in a larger water course).[80] In this way, participants often described the bio-cultural-spatial value of their neighbourhood in relation to the wider city or region and country.

Stage 2 – Harnessing Potential

Regenerative theory seeks to understand potential, arising as it does from the relationship between the uniqueness of a place and the systems within which that place is nested.[81] The connection between uniqueness and potential can be visualised as a rubber band. A rubber band at rest holds two kinds of energy: potential energy, which is stored energy, and kinetic energy, which is energy in motion.[82] When the distance between uniqueness at the place level and potential is stretched too far, making the goal feel impossible to reach, the impulse towards a new direction may lose momentum before becoming realised. If the tension is insufficient, there may be too little motivation to be bring it into existence. By addressing the question 'What could this place really be like if it lived up to its full potential?' participants shifted their way of thinking from dwelling on problems to imagining potentials – and began to view the process of harnessing potential as a source of individual and collective motivation.[83]

Stage 3 – Restraining Forces

Restraining forces were addressed through the '*Law of 3*' regenerative framework, which assumes that three influences need to be present for anything new to be created: the *activating force*, which is endeavouring to create change and bringing innovation; the *restraining force* originating from the receiver of the action and aiming to conserve the status quo; and the *reconciling force*, which endeavours to bring the two forces into relatedness and manifest something new.

By addressing what the restraining forces or challenges are for improving the character of places, the use of green spaces, the level of safety, and how women travel around their areas, participants identified and engaged from a relational perspective with the forces involved in maintaining the status quo in their urban systems.

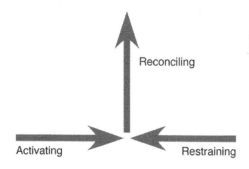

Figure 4: Three forces diagram by Regenesis Group [84]

Stage 4 – Stakeholders Mapping

Stakeholders are usually defined as those who are affected positively or negatively by a project or an initiative. As a result, stakeholder engagement tends to be transactional in nature. From a regenerative design perspective, stakeholder engagement becomes relational. Stakeholders are therefore understood as those who must have a say in realising the potential that a regenerative process brings to their place.[85] By addressing 'Who should be leading these changes?' (originating from the tension between potential and restraining forces), women reflected on the existing social capital present in their areas and distributed relational responsibilities through the system.

Stage 5 – Roles of Women

Since the time of the Greek philosophers of antiquity, many writers and scholars have articulated a deep, intuitive connection between walking and thinking. This stage attempted to create the conditions for participants to reveal, recover and reconsider their roles, positions, and actions as subjects of urban realities. By walking their areas, interviewees explored existing or imagined roles they were prepared to take in order to realise the potential of their place, enhancing the vitality of their green spaces, increasing their active travel choices, and improving perceived and real safety for all.

Stage 6 – Leverage Points

The final stage of the framework of inquiry brings together the previous five – uniqueness, potential, restraining forces, mapping responsibility in the system, and roles of women – towards manifesting leverage points that lead to new lines of work for bridging the gender gap in urban planning.

This book seeks to address the question 'What if Women Designed the City?' from a regenerative perspective. Bear in mind, however, that while regenerative ways of knowing seek to grapple with the task of re-designing our human presence on the planet, I do not claim that the regenerative perspective provides the only valid story for informing the design of gender-sensitive cities.

6 | Mapping Women's 'Presency' through Walking Interviews

'Walking is mapping with your feet. It helps you piece a city together, connecting up neighborhoods that might otherwise have remained discrete entities, different planets bound to each other, sustained yet remote.'
~ Lauren Elkin ~

So much for the theory. To see how cities would look and function if designed by women let us explore how innovative ways of mapping both the presence and agency of contemporary women may support the emergence of previously unrecorded narratives of the city, as perceived by women. My findings are embedded in fieldwork conducted through walking interviews complemented by the use of a GIS* platform used as a tool for storing, managing, visualising, and analysing spatial and nonspatial data.

Walking interviews take place on the move, at the pace and heartbeat of women's daily lives. Involving a 'trialogue' between one or more participants, the place we traversed and myself as a

---

* Geographic Information System - a technology that captures, stores, analyses, and presents geographically referenced data to understand and visualize patterns, relationships, and trends in the real world.

researcher,[86] walking women's neighbourhoods created opportunities for each participant to think aloud, expose their mental models to the open air and engage in an iterative process of reflection between theory and practice.

Walking alongside women while observing and experiencing their everyday practices had multiple benefits. At the outset, participants were able to show rather than describe the aspects of their neighbourhoods associated with themes they wanted to explore, providing me with direct insight into how they perceive, experience and exercise agency in their milieu and vice-versa.

Walking interviews were also dynamically multisensory,[87] engaging with the multiple senses of participants - visual, sound, smell, social and cognitive processes. For instance, several women referred to the relationship between sound and the perceived safety of public space, while another woman interviewed demonstrated how the smell of flowering bushes guided her choice of which pathway to take for her daily commute. Such a multisensory approach already indicates new lines of work on how regenerative design may expand the scope for transforming urban spaces by considering residents' social, cognitive and emotional experiences.

A strength of walking interviews is that they created conditions for serendipitous and unanticipated experiences and insights to emerge.[88] In fact, numerous such events took place, for instance, discussing the consequences of inequitable funding favouring roads over pavements while coming across a father struggling to push a pram/stroller along an uneven path; or talking about large sections of a park as reflecting statements of class, age and gender influence, and being bumped into by a runner representative of such influence; or even being silenced by the loud roar of a car engine while reflecting upon the nuisance of car-centred neighbourhoods.

In the beginning of the 1990s, a version of walking interviews was initiated by the Metropolitan Toronto Action Committee on Violence Against Women and Children's (METRAC) in Canada, as a tool for preventing urban violence as well as increasing women's involvement in city governance.[89] In a 'shape of safety audit', women were invited to walk through the spaces that they use, observing and identifying factors such as inadequate or absent lighting or signage, disheartening graffiti messages, frightening passageways or overgrown bushes which make them feel unsafe.[90] These walks sometimes took place with city officials, after which a report was presented to those responsible for safety in the city. From this point, it was hoped that the recommended changes were implemented, and areas considered threatening became safer places for everyone in the community. The METRAC approach has since been broadened into a general tool to enable decision-makers to gain 'user knowledge' about the city, and vice-versa, for residents to pass their experiences on to the people in charge of urban design.

The walking interviews were participant-driven: that is, participants selected the geographical location and the route for which the interview would unfold. Some participants prepared in advance, while others took a stroll and made decisions where to go in the moment. Women were notified that they were regarded as expert guides and the route they chose would enable me as the researcher to access their experiences and knowledge about the specific area.

Inspired by the participatory self-organising Open Space Technology created by Harrison Owen,[91] I developed simple principles which were easy to grasp and follow.

**What if Women Designed the City Walking Interview Principles
and Golden Rule**

The Three Principles:
1. Women participants are the expert guides choosing the route they
want to explore;
2. Whenever the walk starts is the right time;
3. When it's over, it's over.

The Golden Rule:

Taking part in this interview is voluntary. Choosing not to take part
will not disadvantage you in any way. You have the right and freedom
to withdraw from the walk at any time without explanation.

Table 3: Walking Interview Principles and Golden Rule

Thus, participants made all the decisions including the route to
be followed, the length of time of the walking interview, and
what they wanted to physically show and reveal. The average
length of these walking interviews was one hour; the shortest
being 19 minutes, the longest spanning one hour and 34
minutes. Typically, at the end of each interview, the participants
themselves marked the area walked on an app that I developed
using a GIS platform.

My fieldwork took place at neighbourhood-level in Perth,
Edinburgh and Glasgow. It reached out to 274 women from
both affluent and hard-to-reach neighbourhoods in Perth,
Portobello and Wester Hailes in Edinburgh, and Drumchapel
and Yorkhill & Kelvingrove in Glasgow, to listen to their
reflections on the bio-cultural-spatial uniqueness of their areas.
In responding, they spoke about issues around the accessibility
of social infrastructures, liveliness of green spaces, reliability of
public transport, and safety of their streets. Aspects of the

character of each neighbourhood can be found in the Storyline appendix.

Embedded in their everyday experience of the city, the participating women were invited to reveal existing and potential opportunities for bringing more vitality and viability into the heart of their urban worlds. Their narratives were stimulated by imagining potentiality, identifying restraints and expanding the network of responsibility amongst neighbourhood stakeholders. Unless specified otherwise, all the quotes in the following chapter are drawn from the valuable insights provided by these remarkable women participants.

7 | 33 Leverage Points to Make your City Work Better for Women and Girls

'Being on the fringes of the world is not the best place for someone who wants to re-create it: here again, to go beyond the given, one must be deeply rooted in it.'
~ Simone de Beauvoir ~

The rich findings from my walking interviews provided the context for identifying 33 leverage points and lines of work, contributing towards developing gender-inclusive planning approaches for the regeneration of the neighbourhoods. What follows are these women's generous insights - interwoven with my observations from several cities – that call into question the effectiveness of master planning while gradually envisioning a mosaic of gender-sensitive interventions in their neighbourhoods.

Please be mindful that to apply the concept of leverage points into your city or neighbourhood, finding the right leverage point is only half the journey. The other half concerns activating it in a regenerative direction to cultivate cities that work better for women and girls, as well as for marginalised demographics more broadly.

Leverage Point 1 – Cultivating biophilia

 People are motivated to protect, restore and regenerate places with which they have intimate and meaningful relationships, based on familiarity, knowledge and affection.[92] [93] Cultivating biophilia is a *Mindset* leverage point, where people's sense of identification with living systems is rooted in lived experience.

The word biophilia originates from the Greek, 'philia' meaning 'love of' and bio signifying 'life'.[94] It refers to the inherent bonds humans can form with other species and living systems they rely on. Here, planners and practitioners are invited to grow sensitivities and competences to design spaces in the city where meaningful encounters can take place between humans and other forms of life. Biophilic urban design links pocket parks to burns, allotments to parks, urban woodlands to regional landscapes, providing a continuous experience for residents of all ages – from child to adulthood – to nurture love for living things; and for other living things to move through urban landscapes more freely. This leverage point suggests that by fostering connections between human and more-than-human nature we can support social and ecological systems to co-evolve and thrive.

Inaugurated in 1926,[95] the Parque Garcia Sanabria in Santa Cruz de Tenerife is an excellent example of a park that caters to all ages and invites multiple ways of connecting with nature. Arrive in early morning, and you might join a group of mature women and men dancing their way through the day. Alongside, another group is performing asanas and sun salutations guided by a yoga teacher. And if you arrive at the end of play, you might encounter young women taking selfies and immersing themselves in the scents of the aromatic garden. Elsewhere, boys may be found hiding in the bambooed alcoves. Nearby, benches face one another, as do their occupants. Play spaces interspersed with art forms offer places of discovery for all ages. There is a designed sense of welcome through all entrances to the green space: an invitation to breathe in relaxation and breathe out bio-cultural connectivity. The absence of empty crisp packets, soda cans or any other forms of rubbish, reinforces the fact that positive place identifications can unleash place-protective behaviours and care.

> Stop for a moment. Go inside and bring to mind one of your early memories of being one with an aspect of nature. Fast forward and imagine the same place in the future. How do you imagine it? Hopefully preserved in its inexhaustible vigour.

Regenerative theorist, Carol Sanford, who specialised in systemic business change, believes there is little value in considering the aliveness of living systems solely along intellectual lines.[96] Rather, it should be internalised as a way of being or a way of belonging – as expressed so poetically by Mary Oliver:

> *...Whoever you are, no matter how lonely,*
> *the world offers itself to your imagination,*
> *calls to you like the wild geese, harsh and exciting -*
> *over and over announcing your place*
> *in the family of things.*[97]

During my walking interviews with women in Perth, Scotland, participants demonstrated an affinity for the natural world when speaking about the River Tay. They saw the river preserved as habitat for otters and beavers; alongside carbon-free activities such as sailing, paddle boarding, kayaking; and with a disused hospital building holding the possibility of becoming a wildlife observation centre.

Women proposed that an awakened sense of biophilia cultivated from childhood may help prevent disruptive behaviours during adolescence and the impetus to control and exploit nature in adulthood. Over the years, transformative educators have suggested that children form their values during their early years. Nature is engaged as an integral part of Montessori education, and connecting with nature provides children with many developmental opportunities that staying indoors simply cannot replicate.[98] Maria Montessori believed that each child has an innate love for nature which the developmental psychologist, Jean Piaget, endorsed when suggesting the predisposition of children to explore and bond with the natural world given suitable opportunities and encouragement.[99]

A variety of green-blue spaces available in the city can provide the motivating classrooms for both formal and informal education. Observing patterns in nature, cultivating vegetables and harvesting berries, climbing, swimming, hiding in wild places, the formative years of the current youth growing up in urban settings could foster adults with greater intimacy and respect for the living world. By learning from and with nature – instead of just about nature – children may transcend the anthropocentric cultural limiters they have been born into, and grow up feeling part of, rather than apart from the nested systems that support their and all lives on our planet.

However, it is not only about landscaping and increasing access to existing parks. Women advocated for a more prominent role for nature in urban design; for instance, by enhancing the connection between the surrounding pockets of green with the city centre itself. To achieve this outcome, cities may consider increasing the number and diversity of trees, installing more garden boxes, integrating more rain gardens into streets, and consequently offering more connected and attractive corridors for pollinators, birds and nature lovers. By fostering lively green arteries coursing through our cities, we can place biophilia at the heart of 21st century urbanism.

Leverage Point 2 – Developing spaces for gathering and belonging

 In an equal society, public spaces should be equally accessible and enjoyed by all residents with diverse identities, cultures, physical and mental abilities, and age groups. A recurrent theme that emerged throughout the walking interviews is a sense that the depth and health of relationships between individuals and groups are proportional to the availability of spaces for gathering. A participant suggested 'in the past this space was provided by the churches, but the majority of people in our area no longer go to church'.

It is intriguing how this observation resonated when exploring the historic Sanctuary of San Telmo at the doorway of Triana 'el barrio fino' in Gran Canaria. Inside, the measured pace of a few churchgoers responding to evening prayers in a pre-recorded recital in priestly voice; while outside people of all ages gathered in lively conversations under the trees and around the bustling eateries.

Whilst public green and blue spaces provide meeting points during the day, and restaurants and cafés give ample opportunities to gather over food and drink, women in my interviews argued for the importance of spaces for experiencing together rather consuming individually. In such a way, weather-proof community centres can provide the crucible for socialisation, by welcoming diverse community voices and enabling sense of place to evolve.

Sense of place speaks about meaningful relationships between people and specific locations. It can be understood as 'place identity', when people define themselves as a result of intense interaction with a specific locality.[100] [101] It can also be expressed as 'place attachment', meaning an emotional bond between individuals and their environment – a longing for our place of belonging;[102] or as a 'place of dependence', suggesting that a person or group is attached to a particular place for functional reasons.[103]

> Stop for a moment and reflect about a public space you feel most at ease in. A place where you feel yourself and alive. What does this place mean to you? Now explore what defines your relationship with it. How strongly do you feel you identify with this place? Is this a place where a constellation of social relations has evolved over time, and you may feel distressed being remote from it? Or perhaps this place is unique in meeting your daily needs. Perhaps a combination of aspects?

Sense of place needs a location or physical structure for gatherings to happen, where longing for belonging can be actualised with no expectation that you need to spend money to socialise. The development of easily accessible, democratic spaces for gathering could provide an infrastructure that strengthens community bonds and nurtures sense of place. According to participants of my research, such vibrant, mixed-used, community-managed hubs can be fostered as a result of the cooperation between the public and private sectors and residents' willingness to pool resources.

> In 2017, the membership-led organisation Action Porty in Portobello, Edinburgh, was awarded funds by the Scottish Land Fund to buy the church and halls of Portobello Old Parish Church, with a view of turning it into a multi-purpose community centre. Building upon this effort, a similar collective is involved in re-opening the Town Hall, closed a few years back by the Council. The group hopes it will become a 'venue for all the events of life: weddings and parties, music and dance, markets and sales'. As the urban

population grows and the public sector resources deteriorate, co-developing spaces for gathering strengthens the relationship between stakeholders in the construction of place. It also shifts the quality of association from transactional to relational.

Spaces for gathering is a *Power to add, change and evolve system structure* leverage point. It is grounded in the fact that many women's lives are lived locally, and provides the container for deepening localised everyday experiences for all the community. Speaking to this, an elder from Fairfield housing association in Perth talked about the importance of their neighbourhood centre, as well as the impact of its loss: 'Here in Fairfield we used to go to our community centre on a Tuesday and Wednesday, we had dances, funerals, Christmas parties and a good community spirit. Since its demolition, we retreated to our own houses'.

The vacuum left by the steady closure of social spaces in housing estates across the UK has been filled by agencies, ostensibly acting as a safety net by offering 'programmes' that often fail to reflect what residents genuinely need. They therefore do not effectively contribute to a community's sense of belonging. On this note, an interviewee from Wester Hailes questioned the types of activities the local agencies were promoting: 'Do we actually need a drumming group in this community?'.

Outdoor socialising increased during the Covid-19 pandemic. Women shared concepts for different structures that could serve as outdoor shelters for local gatherings, such as retrofitting disused band stands and purpose-built gazebo-type constructs to hang out in poor weather, offering a comforting and inviting place to draw in people from the periphery to the centre of public spaces.

On the topic of seating arrangements in such public spaces, a woman suggested: 'Some of the benches should be set up in a way that shows that you are happy for people to sit and interact'. While 'happy to chat' benches are by no means a novel idea, they are rarely implemented in public spaces. Indeed, according to one of the women I spoke with, they 'can reduce isolation of those who live by themselves with conversations without being intrusive'. This may seem trifling, but for many women the quality and positioning of benches can turn lonely seats into social spaces and a greater sense of ownership over, and confidence in, the public realm.

Leverage Point 3 – Designing urban extensions while evolving the whole

 Urban extensions refer to new neighbourhoods planned at the edge of existing built-up areas.[104] In my interviews, several women emphasised the importance of moving beyond 'development as usual' to foster a sense of community when designing these urban extensions.

Firstly, to avoid territorial disputes over services, new developments should build their own infrastructure such as telecommunications, waste management, water supply, wastewater, flood risk, and coastal change management integrated into wider urban and regional planning frameworks. Secondly, developments need to make provision for community facilities and amenities such as health centres, education and leisure activities, that contribute to enabling new and existing residents to enjoy, live well and prosper in their area.

This has been the case for Aspern Seestadt neighbourhood, positioned on the outskirts of Vienna and considered one of Europe's largest urban developments with a 'female face'.[105] Incorporating a mixed-use urban design concept, Seestadt is both a residential quarter and a business hub, with about 50% of the area set aside for green spaces including the Janis Joplin Promenade circling the central lake. A study in Vienna found that 4,269 streets memorialise the lives of men, while 356 streets have been named after women.[106] By being named after great women – Hannah Arendt, Simone de Beauvoir, Wangari Maathai – the streets and squares of Seestadt are bridging this gap. A business, science, research, and educational hub combined with a local primary school, a kindergarten focusing on the integration of children with special needs – all facilities reduce the emphasis on daily commuting and create the conditions for localisation of daily life. With well-being at the heart of the district, GPs, specialist medical practitioners, therapists and pharmacists provide healthcare to the community, in the community.

What can Portobello in Edinburgh learn from Seestadt? As its popularity increases, the pressure for Portobello to grow increases, incorporating adjacent brownfield land from the industrial and commercial Seafield area. Women discussed the need to avoid a 'development as usual' approach for this potential extension. Firstly, they believe developers should listen to women's perspectives and knit together the subtleties of the areas in order to successfully expand the sense of community. This could be done through making sure construction materials and methods demonstrate a connection to local history and culture.

As a clear demonstration of the leverage point *Power to add, change, evolve or self-organise system structure,* women suggested making the edges between areas more dynamic by crafting paths that meander between buildings, through and around vegetation and beneath smart lighting where new residents can 'feel' they are still within Portobello. They went further, proposing that services should evolve as a whole to include a comprehensive recycling scheme and expanded services on the beach with accessible and regularly cleaned toilets, beach huts and showers benefitting new and existing developments.

Yorkhill & Kelvingrove in the West-End of Glasgow is known for its famous hospitals. When the Sick Children Hospital was relocated from Garnethill to Yorkhill in 1914, it occurred against a background of tough living conditions, with children being raised in overcrowded slum tenements, and an infant mortality rate amongst the highest in Europe.[107] Fifty years on, the Queen Mother's Maternity Hospital opened on a site adjacent to the Royal Hospital for Sick Children, establishing a national centre for integrated obstetrics and paediatric healthcare.[108] During my research, I spoke with numerous nurses who moved into the area in the 1970s to work in the hospital, which at that time was known as 'the Mother and Baby Hospital'. One participant highlighted how the establishment of the hospital led to the transformation of the area from a working-class to a white-collar neighbourhood, evidenced by the number of nurses residing in the vicinity.

Today, following a notable increase in visitors, the upsurge in the construction of student accommodation and a recent increase in the number of local businesses, Yorkhill & Kelvingrove is becoming one of the most desirables places to live in Glasgow. On the one hand, developers want to develop as many one-bedroom flats as they can to meet and expand market demand; on the other hand, through a process of lower-class displacement, long-term residents and tenants are substituted for more affluent incomers, attracted by the place's 'hipster' identity and wealth of art, parklands, independent shops, and colonial-era architecture.

Those who oppose this process of gentrification advocate for creating more co-housing developments and for keeping current and long-term residents and families in the area, which they believe will continue to strengthen the collective experience of belonging to Yorkhill & Kelvingrove and preserve its authenticity. In cases where re-development is practically inevitable – such as the plans for developing the former hospital site – the women I interviewed advocated for preserving local character and community identity. They suggested achieving this by ensuring architectural consistency in terms of style, materials, and construction methods between buildings of the past and future constructions.

In summary, this leverage point could inform a 'how-to' manual for developers when planning for urban extensions seeking to:

1- foster more dynamic edges between areas;

2- design such that the original area evolves and benefits from (re)development;

3- plan for adequate amenities and facilities to avoid placing any additional stress on the area;

4- make sure construction materials and methods connect with culture, memory and history;

5- promote active travel routes to connect the areas and enhance community belonging;

6- assign female names for new streets – after all many more streets are named after men than women. Why not use new developments as part of a rebalancing effort?

Leverage Point 4 – Shifting from a mentality of maintenance to an attitude of care

Shifting mindsets from a mentality of maintenance to an attitude of care is one of the most fundamental *Goals of the system* leverage points. This was reaffirmed by the women I spoke to who viewed this shift as having great potential for addressing the level of brokenness they experienced in their cities and neighbourhoods. Political scientist, Joan Tronto, defines care as 'everything that we do to maintain, continue, and repair "our world" so that we can live in it as well as possible. That world includes our bodies, ourselves, and our environment, all of which we seek to interweave in a complex, life sustaining web'.[109]

In the UK, problems with the maintenance and upkeep of urban green spaces are more likely to occur in hard-to-reach communities than affluent areas.[110] Sadly, funding cuts and spatial discrimination advance hand-in-hand, with women reporting high levels of neglect in green spaces in Wester Hailes and Drumchapel. Nevertheless, women saw potential for establishing a culture of alliances between local authorities, housing associations and communities, with the task of caring for public space, benefitting quality of life of all.

In Drumchapel, women who experience a constant decline in the quality of their built environment alluded to the potential for caring for what is already there. They were adamant about the need to renew their relationship with the spirit of place, absent since the urban planners of the 1960s engineered the area. Facing a new wave of regeneration guided by the 20-minute neighbourhood framework, they wished to turn their open spaces, considered unattractive and uninviting, into revitalised places of social interaction. For four years these women have wanted to redevelop a closed Pavilion into a community hub with a café, if only the local authority would alleviate bureaucratic and regulatory hindrances. They want to see regeneration beyond housing upgrades and transform their bleak environments into a mosaic of community projects led by people who care for things not because they produce value, but because they are already valued by the community.

A woman from Wester Hailes spoke about the 'tarmac strategy', adopted by those in charge of 'maintaining' play areas and green spaces: 'There was a period of time whenever you turned around, they tarmacked another piece'. The flawed rationale behind this has been that 'tarmac makes things look tidy and better, because the bushes get out of hand'. To this, the woman jokingly surmised that 'the Council decided the best way to look after the green space was not to have any'. Photos of Wester Hailes genesis can be found in legendary community-activist periodical, *The Sentinel*, which shows the area dominated by high-rise blocks of flats separated by wide extents of concrete and tarmac. Over the years the tarmac approach has continued to reign supreme.

A Word of Warning!

In this discussion we need to be mindful that responsibility for improving neighbourhoods doesn't fall on women purely because of gender stereotypes which often limit women's realities to the heroic role of caregiver. Thus, distribution of such responsibilities should be equitable and combined with sincere open interactions, actively inviting all stakeholders into discussions to find and implement new lines of work. This avoids locking the responsibility of care solely in the hands of women.

Poor maintenance sends a simple but graphic message of 'we don't care'. That is how some women view the shortfall in garbage collection services in the Yorkhill & Kelvingrove area, with nothing more unwelcoming than seeing messy, rubbish-strewn streets. Indeed, a group of women frequenting the Om

Hindu Mandir temple stated that the bins at the corner of their temple are constantly overflowing, negatively impacting the feeling of well-being in their place of worship. These women were adamant regarding the need to thoroughly rethink bins on the streets. But what can be done?

While maintenance is about working on what already exists from an operational perspective, care as we refer to it here is concerned with improving systems through relational means. A Department of Care within a municipality could, for instance, enquire into 'how we best accomplish this urban improvement within available, shared resources?' Residents may engage in participatory budgeting (a process in which citizens are involved in deciding how public money is spent), enabling stakeholders to do more with less – in particular, utilising local labour and materials to reduce reliance on fossil-fuel based products and long supply chains.

Since its creation in 2005, the Col·lectiu Punt 6 cooperative of architects, sociologists and urban planners in Barcelona have promoted the notion of the 'caring city' – where care of people is at the centre of planning decisions, without pigeonholing women as the carers. Instead, they propose that care must be a collective responsibility. They prefer the term 'caring city' to the concept inclusive cities, which reaffirms the permanent existence of the other that needs to be included.[111] [112]

If the goal of the system (of your city) is to bring about different ways of dealing with the brokenness of the urban fabric, a series of facilitating mechanisms may be put in place such as distribution of care responsibilities, removal of unnecessary red tape and participatory allocation of budget lines. Women believe 'care' needs to be nurtured and democratised, involving residents in discussions on how it can be optimally distributed in conjunction with local authorities in their role of supporting, structuring and synergising this process. This leverage point highlights the role that care giving and receiving can play in the repairability of our broken world. After all, as American writer and management consultant, Margaret J Wheatley, so astutely remarked: 'there is no power for change greater than a community discovering what it cares about'.[113]

Leverage Point 5 – Redistributing land use and budget allocation for equality and gendered landscapes

 Indian ecofeminist and food sovereignty activist, Vandana Shiva, asserts that we create the context for what we measure.[114] This line of work falls within the *Rules of the system* via *Parameters* leverage point. It arises from the observation that traditionally male competitive sports dominate the allocation of land in green spaces, compared with land dedicated for non-competitive activities. In other words, sports opportunities are not a level playing field.

In the process of data collection, participants declared that the future depends on cooperation between decision-makers and communities. Cooperation in this context refers to designing to increase rather than limit women, girls and children's options in green spaces. It includes designing to support less confident groups – young girls, people with health conditions or impairments, and the elderly – to stake a claim to their green areas. For instance, an elderly participant recounted that 'going up or down this park path while pushing my late husband's wheelchair was a nightmare and quite dangerous', as the steep and slippery slope on wet days did not allow for a gradual change in direction. She understood that this has to do with cost-cutting measures, as installing straight line pathways are cheaper than zigzagging and meandering ones.

Children and young people must be consulted when planning and redesigning green spaces, particularly young girls who will become regular park users. This has been successfully done in Umeå, Sweden, which is recognised as a model city for gender responsive urban planning and mobility.[115] Umeå promotes collaboration between the municipality and groups of girls, resulting in its exemplary 'gendered landscape', supporting young girls to take their place confidently in the public sphere.[116] The city's planning practice demonstrates the co-evolving mutualism concept in action, where young girls shape the form of the city while the city supports their freedom to move, socialise and be themselves.

Is participation enough? Not according to Donnella Meadows, who suggested that when attempting to understand system malfunctions, it is essential to pay attention to the rules, and to who has power over them.[117]

Ensuring that the right to open green space is more evenly distributed, requires those who hold power within local government to measure the area dedicated to male dominated sports, and formulate policy and planning guidelines to address the gendered imbalances in green space planning and use.

Planning guidelines could promote combining smaller-scale and larger-scale sub-zones in green spaces, better balancing multiple users and uses. Within this framework, older generations should be allocated protected, shady spaces with visual axes to more lively zones of green spaces, strengthening links of belonging and enhancing their sense of self-worth. Such an approach has been implemented in Vienna's Rudolf-Bednar-Park, designing the greenspace to include tranquil zones in the form of neighbourhood gardens, gender-balanced sports zones, areas for play and exercise for all age groups and a footpath network to allow for circular walking routes in the park.[118]

Continuing with leverage points to transform the unequal distribution of green space, there is a need to allocate budget lines to widen the repertoires of activities catering for women and girls' needs. This has been effectively done in Lyon – the largest French city to implement a gender-sensitive budget – ensuring, for instance, that womens' sports clubs receive as many subsidies as men's'.[119] Officials in Lyon view the gendered budget as a transformative instrument addressing societal inequalities – a gap that has become even more pronounced since the Covid-19 pandemic. In fact, there is a gender-responsive budget revolution spreading across cities in Europe. Known as *Budget-Genré* in France and *Presupuesto con Enfoque de Género* (PEG) in Spain, gender-responsive budgets adopt principles for gender equality as a framework for making decisions in all phases of the budget cycle.

Spain has been using gender-responsive budgeting in its national and sub-national administrative budgets since 2007. The Andalusian Regional Government Administration, for instance, has developed and implemented a specific methodology – the G+ Programme – to classify all programmes on the extent to which they impact on gender.[120] So far, the G+ Programme has seen an expansion of after-school services for children, a rise in women's ownership of agricultural holdings, a greater focus on combating violence against women, and an increase in female university professors from 13% in 2008 to 20% in 2015.

Former US President Barak Obama asserted that 'a budget is more than just a series of numbers on a page; it is an embodiment of our values'.[121] The participatory budgeting methodology invented in Porto Alegre and since adopted in many cities around the world,[122] is a manifestation of genuine citizen engagement, prioritising what is needed and meaningful at their local level. To make green spaces equally inviting for and engaged in by women, there is a need to challenge the rules of the system (and those who hold them). We can do this by measuring the amount of land dedicated to competitive sports and addressing the inequities we find, and putting budgets to work to reflect the values of gendered landscapes that widen the space and repertoires of physical activities available for women and girls.

Leverage Point 6 – Creating conditions for wildness

  How to increase the proportion of land given over to a wilder, less cultivated state (*Parameters* leverage point), and the acceptance of wildlife's right to evolve and diversify (*Power to add, change, evolve or self-organise a system structure* leverage point), was a recurrent theme in my walking interviews.

Urban re-wilding is a disputed notion which often refers to the science-based restoration of self-regulating ecosystems and to a transformation in human-nature relationships.[123] However, the human-nature dichotomy is a Western construct that has led to narrowly utilitarian and exploitative relationships with many other species, effectively driving the 6th Mass Extinction on Earth.[124] For many of the First People indigenous communities of Brazil, my home country, the human-nature concept does not exist. Yanomami girls can recite over 200 names of flora encountered in their Amazonian home;[125] while a girl raised in London, may have to visit Kew Gardens to readily experience such floral diversity and develop their botanical knowledge.

Encouraging such eco-literacy, a participant from Portobello in Edinburgh shared her experience of creating willow tunnels and planting wildflowers with kids in Figgate Park, who experienced a strong sense of nature connection and participation. Another suggested a combination of wild meadows and orchards, encouraging natural growth and harvesting, not only for humans but for birds, bees and insects – allowing some areas to become self-willed land again.

Originally the citadel of Lille designed by Vauban in the 1660s was constructed to use the swamp water and mud as a natural defence to make conditions more difficult for any invading force besieging the citadel.[126] Through a system of locks and water gates, 1,700 hectares around the citadel could be flooded to a depth of 55 cm. Today the 110 hectares park surrounding the citadel developed on marshland at the junction of the rivers Deûle and Bucquet, is a great example of a self-willed landscape. When the century-old oaks, hornbeams and beeches perish, they are left to decompose on site or piled and mounted with various cavities to serve as shelters for hedgehogs, weasels, foxes, and many other *petites bêtes*. Sheep graze on the slopes of the fortifications, keeping the vegetation trimmed and replacing the motorised equipment otherwise required. Not far from Lille in Valenciennes, the authorities have been notified of a 'massive feline' roaming the area in the evenings.[127] Depending on the strong winds blowing as I walked the citadel park, my sense of smell picked up the presence of *bêtes*, both *petites* and *grandes*. This feels like urban re-wilding.

In Scotland, a group of volunteers and 'wildlife spotters' from Yorkhill Green Spaces[128] in Glasgow have been improving the wildflower meadows of Yorkhill Park, repopulating the West End green spaces with insects and compiling a biodiversity inventory now encompassing 1,174 species. The group facilitates volunteers and students to plant bulbs in the autumn and wildflowers in spring, providing habitat for pollinators. In the same area, another initiative provides a 'learning landscape', for children to experience foraging and exploration of hidden places at the edge of the built environment and the railway lines. A woman interviewee described 'a very dark and dingy park' which has been upgraded by the community themselves who subsequently became active users, carers and biodiversity enhancers. Many people who lived in the area did not know it existed until it was revitalised.

There have also been attempts by local authorities in the area to promote the 20-minutes neighbourhood concept, which asserts that 20 minutes should be the upper limit people should be required to walk to meet their daily needs – and therefore contributing to the push towards net-zero.[129] This is discussed further in Leverage Point 24.

The potential for integrating the concepts of rewilding and 20-minute neighbourhoods is immense – from providing food forests and habitats for wildlife and enhancing green corridors to link together habitat fragments within and between neighbourhoods, to enabling people to recognise nature's importance and foster a sense of co-evolving mutualism with the natural world. Rewilding 20-minute neighbourhoods could also reduce the costs of, and on occasions the need for green space management-as-usual practices such as mowing, weeding and applying pesticides. Furthermore, green spaces can be effectively encouraged to better retain and distribute excess rainwater, reduce air pollution and sequester carbon, making areas more resilient to flooding and heat waves.

Within the siloed cultures of our city services, urban rewilding can constitute an important shared conversation between departments within local authorities. This could proceed under a multi-stakeholder umbrella, potentially named 'Rewilding 20-minute Neighbourhoods', and charged with creating conditions for wildlife to thrive, where the diversity of species evolves rather than stagnates or declines, and the interconnectedness of humans and our fellow species can be experienced by and for all.

Leverage Point 7 – Devising a library of women-tailored bike saddles

 Cycling gets you further, faster and healthier. However, across the UK, US and Canada, two-wheeled commuting is largely dominated by men.[130] Indeed, just 11% of women in the UK cycle at least once a week, compared to 23% of men.[131] Research has continuously emphasised that this is mainly due to lack of protective infrastructure, leaving women feeling unsafe to cycle.[132] [133]

This leverage point is not about infrastructural factors such as improving city lights and implementing segregated bike lanes, or even the cultural factors that place expectations on women to arrive at work 'respectably dressed'. Rather, and perhaps surprisingly to many, it is on how to promote enough debate and awareness around the health implications that inappropriate saddles and ill-fitting bikes can have on women's bodies, particularly in the vulval area.

As women typically possess wider hips, ischial bones and smaller bodies, they generally benefit from wider saddles, allowing us to avoid injuries caused by pressure placed on the front of the genital area.[134] The soft tissue in the perineum is not structured to bear weight, particularly when bent-over assuming a riding position.[135] Speaking to this, a participant recommended that bicycle shops develop a library of women-tailored saddles designed to respond to women's anatomy, making cycling a more comfortable experience.

How can cycling become safer for all women? Women I spoke to argued that options should not be limited to two wheelers: 'tricycles can be really good for women, who may worry about tipping [over] while taking lots of stuff, your weekly shop, or even your dog'.

Awareness of potential injuries, and the promotion of a comfortable culture of cycling for women and girls, needs to start 'when you are really young, so that you can grow in confidence as you age'. A long-term Scandinavian resident of Edinburgh, who has never owned a car and whose parents never gave her a lift to school, parties, or extra-curricular activities, argued that 'cycling has to start at school. It is a societal thing more than an infrastructure'.

Finding 'the right saddle that fits your bottom and supports your weight' should be a priority for all women cyclists, young or more mature, whether taking a long commute or enjoying a recreational trip. This leverage point is about crossing the threshold of what the author of *Invisible Women*, Caroline Criado Perez, calls the 'male default thinking' [136] which seem too often to inform the decisions of designers of bicycles and tricycles. Ergonomically-appropriate saddles should respond to different women's anatomies and offer a wide diversity of bicycle seats in shops everywhere. As an *Information flow* leverage point, poetic and unswerving messages such as this Haiku should inspire designers, retailers and users to foster the emergence of a culture of female cyclists in cities, where women are active travel protagonists.

She rides her bike
Effortless by true saddle
Oh – just a tailwind

Leverage Point 8 – Growing and foraging for health and wellbeing

 Increasingly, our food and medicine are flown to us from across the globe. Supermarkets in the global north tend to be stocked with fruit and vegetables from all corners of the Earth. Health food shops are stocked with 'superfoods' from threatened ecosystems, and we are commonly offered critically endangered species such as *Arnica montana* sold as a balm for our bruises and muscle aches, declining in both quality and area in its native grasslands of Central Europe.[137]

For the UN Food and Agriculture Organization (FAO), the globalisation of our food systems distributing highly processed, high-calorie and low nutritional food items, has had a worldwide impact on food security, health and general well-being.[138] This leverage point relates to the role of women in advancing the localisation of food systems through regenerative practices. It concerns the power to evolve food systems, whereby the social and health relevance of growing and foraging for food in urban settings contributes to cutting food miles and decolonising our plates. It speaks to the words of the indigenous elder, Davi Kopenawa Yanomami in Brazil,[139] who once stated that: 'If I eat white people's food, I have cowboy dreams'.

The women I interviewed for my research spoke about re-establishing connection with their landscape, history and local ways of cultivating plants that grow in their localities. The UK's tradition of allotments has its roots in the industrialisation period of the 19th century when land was allocated by local authorities to the poor to enable them to grow their own food. The allotment culture grew and consolidated during the World War years.[140] Currently, in the cities of Edinburgh, Perth and London, there is typically a seven to ten year wait before a plot is allocated.[141] Women I interviewed in these cities expressed their desire to expand existing food growing activities to improve health, social connectivity, as well as reduce food miles and the cost of living.

Women from Perth, for instance, suggested that the city should aim to be recognised as an urban gateway to a wider agricultural region which seeks to care for the environment. They stated that as 'veganism and healthy lifestyles are a growing market, Perth has the potential to connect its farming roots, farmers markets, grow-your-own and veganism trends for the benefit of its citizens' health and well-being'.

In the context of healthy eating, a woman from the modernist housing estate of Wester Hailes, Edinburgh, mentioned that 'people in this area like hamburgers, pizzas, mashed potatoes and stuff like that'. Encouraging more community gardens could potentially support residents to eat healthier and 'get rid of microwave meals while they taste what they can grow'. Another Wester Hailes local resident recognised the social benefits that creating new community gardens might have for the area, as they can bring people together as a community and counter the reality that 'many people live a solitary life'. For instance, the regular community meals using produce from the Murrayburn and Hailes Neighbourhood Garden attract many people who live on their own and constitutes a place where they can go 'even if they don't want to talk'. Indeed, one participant from Wester Hailes highlighted how community meals hosted at the Edible Estates allotments[142], are especially 'good for people who are slightly depressed'. This speaks to research that suggests that by getting our hands into the soil, a specific soil bacteria, *Mycobacterium vaccae*, triggers the release of the natural anti-depressant serotonin, which in turn can help people to feel more relaxed and happier.[143] [144] This is complemented by compelling evidence on how 'green care' such as social and therapeutic horticulture, care farming and environmental conservation, is beneficial for individuals with mental health challenges, contributing to a reduction in levels of anxiety, stress, and depression.[145]

Nature-based Health Carers

Several women narrated their experiences of being referred by their doctors to the Wester Hailes Community Herbal Clinic at the Health Agency. The Clinic offers patients free medicine but incentivises them to grow the herbs themselves. Supported by the Grass Roots Remedies workers cooperative,[146] there is a developing network of women who meet on a regular basis at the community-led Calders garden to exchange experience alongside growing, foraging and making their own medicine. Currently, there are many community gardens around the area which hold the potential to establish more herbal gardens and thus reach a wider spectrum of households, particularly those who live in flats and have no access to private gardens.

In many cities around the world women play a crucial role in household food production, growing vegetables in gardens and vacant urban spaces. In the boroughs of New York City (NYC) there is a lively ecosystem of women urban farmers, non-profit leaders, dietitians, and chefs committed to localising food systems while serving the most vulnerable. While health food options are often found in the affluent areas such as in Upper East Side Manhattan (many cultivating their vegetable and herbs utilising aeroponics systems on their rooftops), this need is particularly relevant in low-income neighbourhoods dominated by fast-food restaurants. In the Bronx, residents are coming together to establish community gardens to encourage access to fresh, chemical-free produce that they would otherwise have to travel outside the borough to find.[147] Young women from Black, Indigenous, and People of Colour (BIPOC) urban farmers' communities in NYC believe that 'like fashion, farming is political too'.[148] Some have built their capacity through courses at the Farm School NYC, which provides them with the participatory tools they need to become effective leaders in the food justice movement.[149]

There are multiple ways to describe the capacity of a system to change and reinvent itself. Women's vital role as growers and foragers has largely been neglected by city officials, urban planners and developers. Women, as responsible consumers, believe they must also be in some way producers. This potential can be unleashed by releasing allotment space from vacant lots and development sites for community gardening and creation of herbal medicine kitchens. This can also be achieved through regulatory measures by linking planning approval of new developments to the provision of open space for garden cultivation, either on-site or within the neighbouring area. In cities, growing and foraging together deepens social links, encourages more diversified diets, minimises food miles, and promotes radical community healthcare.

Leverage Point 9 – Designing adventurous playgrounds for children and carers

 The UN Convention on the Rights of the Child article 31 states: 'every child has the right to rest, relax, play and to take part in cultural and creative activities'.[150] The women I spoke to in three Scottish cities were eager to promote equity in play spaces across their cities, so that children of all abilities and across all socio-economic backgrounds could access the play equipment they need to thrive.

Accessible play equipment varies according to neighbourhood. A village green space might have only one harness swing, while a large park may have a choice of swinging equipment, wheelchair roundabout and trampolines. Having limited play equipment can prove exclusionary, as one woman with a disabled daughter reflected: 'It is alright for 5 minutes but essentially you are strapping a child into a swing and then isolating her from everybody else'. She continued on to state that what her daughter really wants is to play with the other children on the climbing frames. This suggests a *Power to add, change, evolve or self-organise system structure* leverage point addressing how to evolve play areas towards equitable use for children with a wide variety of abilities.

One contribution to this could be designing similar equipment offering different levels of challenge and grouping them together so that children of different abilities can take part in the same type of activity in close proximity to each other. Speaking on the proximity of play equipment, one of the women I interviewed praised the location of the play park next to the skate park at Kelvingrove in Glasgow, which allowed siblings with an age gap to play in the same area. According to her, this example could be extended to all cities.

Research has highlighted how play is important and often overlooked in adulthood.[151] [152] [153] One woman pointed out how parents in the UK often stand outside play areas, getting chilly while waiting for their kids. She recommended offering opportunities for parental engagement, drawing inspiration from play parks in Germany. This would require the installation of appropriate infrastructure such as 'big wooden climbing frames', which allow parents to become involved and play with their children. Examples given include placing swings in trees for grown-ups and children, which were installed and became 'popular during the pandemic but were taken down sadly because of health and safety issues'.

'In the late 1970s and early 1980s, a series of wooden structures (Adventure Playgrounds) affectionately called the Venchies were built by the local community in Wester Hailes after concern that there was nowhere for children to play in the immediate area. The Venchies were in many ways ahead of their time, as there is now great interest in play areas that provide unstructured play with a degree of challenge. Sadly, the Venchies were short lived becoming unsafe due to a lack of resources to maintain and supervise them, and they were all demolished by 1990.'[154]

A number of women raised concerns around play parks being made too safe, taking away their adventurous edge, with one stating 'don't try to save our children, as they learn when making mistakes'. This sentiment is backed up by studies that have found that children who had improved their motor skills in playgrounds from an early age were less likely to suffer accidents as they got older.[155] [156] The charity Play England has argued that even when risks are taken and injuries occur, in many instances such experiences have a positive role in child development.[157] The problem, according to one of the women, can be embedded by design, because 'sometimes, city planning is too geared for safety'.

If we want our children to be prepared for risk, we need to allow them the space to take risks they can learn from, and in doing so gain the confidence to take some responsibility for the consequences of their choices. This leverage point concerns evolving the sanitised playground trilogy of swing, seesaws and slides to become play spaces which offer more diverse, creative and profound play experiences for different abilities and ages. It is about participatory play where carers and children enjoy the same spaces together, encouraging mutual freedom. It is also about creating playable neighbourhoods for everyone, with the power to promote a play culture that embraces a more holistic understanding of and approach to risk.

Leverage Point 10 – Working with men to redistribute power, balance representation and transform legal and planning systems

 Promoting 'safety in cities' sits at the heart of SDG 11, which aims to 'make cities inclusive, safe, resilient and sustainable'; and more specifically in indicator SDG 11.7.2, measuring 'the proportion of persons victim of physical or sexual harassment, by sex, age, disability status and place of occurrence'. According to the UN SDG metadata repository, indicator 11.7.2 is characterised as Tier II, meaning it is conceptually clear, has an internationally established methodology and standards are available, but data is not regularly produced by countries.

Data disaggregation is important because the act of counting people shows that they count. The lack of disaggregated data clearly indicates that in many cities around the world, planners and decision makers are operating in an environment of ambiguity, creating policies and allocating resources for safety interventions without a clear understanding of the needs, perceptions and demands of women and girls. How can we bridge this gap?

Firstly, we need a *glocal** consensus that the rights of women are integral to safety strategies. Faced with a legal system and cultural context that fails to stem unwanted 'sexualised remarks and gestures from male strangers', one woman claimed that the existing laws are ineffective, and introducing new ones doesn't solve the problem because the system was created long ago by men for their own advantage. To change the system we need to

---

* A term that combines the words 'global' and 'local' and emphasises the interconnectedness of local and global contexts, encouraging the adaptation of global ideas and practices to local circumstances.

change the culture, which 'doesn't happen by tweaking the legislation, which means putting new content in old bottle, and that which is old also needs to be transformed'.

Street-level sexual harassment is a form of behaviour that involves acts to degrade or humiliate a person in a public place.[158] In the UK, harassment is both a criminal offence and a civil action under the Protection from Harassment Act 1997.[159] In other words, someone can be prosecuted in the criminal courts for harassment, and women can also take action against the person in the civil court if harassed. However, several women I spoke to challenged the validity of the law as 'an incredibly blunt tool', as it places responsibility on women to denounce a behaviour that should not have occurred in the first place. 'Legally, things need to change' asserted a mother as she strolled alongside her two daughters in Edinburgh. Reflecting on the consequences of the criminalisation path, she continued: 'the guys leave the system still believing they have not done anything wrong and that they have been victim of the justice system'. A cultural shift towards making misogynistic behaviour completely unacceptable must be promoted, rather than solely pursuing a criminalisation approach. This means challenging structures which reinforce male privilege to redistribute power, balance representation and ensure the overt dismissal of women's experiences are restored into the legal and planning systems. It constitutes a *Goal of the system* leverage point held within a co-evolving mutualism perspective, which intentionally avoids a zero-sum universe where women's gain is men's loss.

The roles that women and men assume in the city need to be rebalanced, until women are no longer viewed or treated as 'the other'.[160] The women in my research spoke of urban realities where they no longer experience misogynistic innuendos and abuses from youth to maturity. As one woman put it, 'we are on a journey for future generations'.

How to empower this journey in practical terms? Some women were motivated to reclaim the streets in groups by engaging in evening activities, marking the places that feel threatening and rendering them more visible – as was successfully done by women in Ontario engaged with the transformative work of METRAC.[161] Indeed, one woman asserted that such interventions may not change the dynamic of places from one day to the next, but can generate stories to drive more substantive and effective conversations with men in the area. Reinforcing this point, women identified the need to communicate with men and make them more aware of the impact of their behaviour, including asking them probing questions such as 'what if that woman was your daughter?' Others suggested campaigning on the basis that 'harassment is not a compliment', until every street in every city becomes safe for women, regardless of the time of day.

Leverage Point 11 – Building confidence through easy-to-access self-defence training, and seminars on rights of women and domestic violence

 There is a subtle difference between perceived safety, which refers to a fear arising from judgements concerning the possibility of being harmed or suffering loss, and feeling unsafe as a direct experience of being harmed. For some women, feeling safe is attributed to personal confidence. Women from different cities referred to an inner strength that supports them to walk the streets fearlessly, stating that: 'I grew up in this sort of environment and understand the sea and the city', or 'I'm pretty dobbie, not easily intimidated'. By being 'quite a confident person' or knowing 'how to keep myself safe' and avoiding 'doing silly things like go down a dark alley way', the women I walked with described how they are able to respond to unusual edgy encounters without giving way to nerves.

Self-confidence is an ability that can be developed and strengthened over time and through life circumstances. This was thoroughly demonstrated by the women I met from housing estates in Edinburgh, Glasgow and Perth, who displayed mental fortitude, resolve, and inventiveness in getting to grips with the state of safety in their areas. Over the decades they have developed survival protocols, from training in self-defence to knowing where and when to go out.

Interactions on the streets of their neighbourhoods can be intimidating. Women mentioned frightening encounters, particularly with those under the influence of drugs, and how in such encounters they avoided gazing so as not to attract attention, as some people can suddenly become very aggressive, shouting 'what are you looking at?' One woman commented that there were lots of angry people in her community making her feel unsafe; while another mentioned the violence that goes on in homes, with women emerging with black eyes or couples under the influence of drugs where the man is visibly dominating his partner.

The potential for women to be who they wish to be and defend themselves emerged from such conversations, with one young woman stating that 'women need to be ready for a fight!' In such contexts, self-defence training is viewed as widening women's options to recognise, prevent, and interrupt violence against them or others.[162] This can be encouraged through practising simple techniques adapted for women's bodies and capacities through martial arts training, as well as acquiring suitable verbal, psychological, and emotional skills.[163]

Women's self-defence training has been criticised for not addressing the underlying factors of harassment and violence, and for giving women a false sense of safety.[164] However, for several of the research participants this has not held true. Unlike much of the safety advice which limits a woman's freedom, particularly during the evenings, self-defence has boosted their confidence to go out and helped them to transition from acting out of fear to embracing boldness. As such, one of my interviewees argued the need for more funding for self-defence classes, which should take place regularly with 'refreshers, every year or six months'. Putting on mixed gender martial arts classes was proposed, as a way to both build women's capacity and teach men more about boundaries and respect for women.

I also heard diverse voices suggesting that their communities need to take domestic violence more seriously, rather than view it as social taboo that is rarely talked about. They believe there should be more encouragement for women to contact the police, particularly those who come from other cultural backgrounds and who may not be aware of the rules of the land. One participant emphasised that each woman should know their human rights to equality, dignity and bodily integrity and act promptly if their life or sense of safety is ever in jeopardy. For this to happen, seminars on the rights of women and on domestic violence should be offered to everybody, delivering information, building capacity, and providing an informed and embodied understanding of violence.

Both training in self-defence and seminars on women's rights can be viewed as capacity building activities relating to the *Structure of information flows* leverage point, where the rights of women must be positioned as integral to safety strategies. Those proposing this leverage point are aligned to the essence of Anna Laetitia Barbauld's epic *'The Rights of Woman'* poem penned in 1793: 'Yes, injured Woman! Rise, assert thy right!'.[165]

Leverage Point 12 – Improving natural surveillance by design

 Natural surveillance refers to a basic principle: if potential offenders believe they might be seen, they are less likely to offend. Thus, it acts as an effective deterrent for those considering criminal activity. Natural surveillance proceeds in two ways. First, you have the presence of passers-by performing the role of 'the eyes on the street'.[166] Also known as 'passive surveillance', this perspective alleges that the safest places in cities are ones that are under constant observation by other people.[167] A word of caution, however! Areas filled with activity can also provide cover for criminals to feel sufficiently anonymous to act – as is the case of pickpockets operating in the beautiful Sultanahmet Square, surrounded by the Blue Mosque, Hagia Sophia and Museum of Turkish and Islamic Arts, in Istanbul. And whilst the 'eyes on the street' was highlighted as one of the major reasons behind the sense of safety, not all found it comforting. One woman stressed 'I don't want to be watched but I want to be safe'.

Not all streets offer the same sense of safety. Unless you live in Greenwich Village in New York or Le Marais in Paris, where the eyes on the street can be present on every block, neighbourhoods tend to be composed of an ecosystem of streets with different functions. From main streets and boulevards to avenues, residential streets, shared-surface streets, alleyways, and arcades, the roles of these different street types are as diverse as their ever-changing users.

Therefore, 'eyes on the street' must be complemented with a second, design-led natural surveillance measure. Such an approach is based on the assumption that by designing built environments or signage in a way that maximises visibility and people's ability to be seen through surrounding windows, transport hubs and retail sites, wrongdoing is discouraged.[168]

Known as 'Crime Prevention Through Environmental Design' (CPTED) the 'design for crime resilience' approach has gained considerable significance worldwide since the 1980s.

The combination of 'eyes on the street' and 'designing out crime', is a leverage point related to reinforcing *Feedback loops* relative to the impacts both measures attempt to correct. Despite their presence not always being very obvious, for many these combined measures can be more effective than technology-enhanced surveillance such as CCTV and panic buttons in parks, bus stops and on university campuses, which don't always make women feel safer. In fact, several women did not regard CCTV as effective in preventing random acts of harassment and violence against residents. Despite the intent of such surveillance systems, CCTV appears to symbolise the opposite of what is intended: 'When I see a camera, I think this is possibly an unsafe place'.

Indore, Hyderabad, and New Delhi are some of the most surveilled cities in the world. For every 1,000 people, Indore has 62.52 cameras coming in second only to Chinese cities like Shanghai, Beijing, and Chongqing, which have 372.8 cameras per 1,000 persons. Does this make women feel safer? Movements like 'Women Walk at Midnight', who have been gathering women to walk the streets of Delhi and Bangalore since 2018, do not think so.[169] Founded by the theatre *artivist**, Mallika Taneja, the movement considers walking as a 'profoundly political act' in deconstructing the unspoken patriarchal rule which implies that women must avoid walking the streets alone at night. Women who participate in these walks are conscious of the constant surveillance that follows their every step and for them

---

* An individual who combines art and activism, referring to the use of artistic expression as a form of advocacy and social change.

CCTV cameras may have helped in collecting evidence after a crime has occurred, but not in preventing it.

Certainly, architecture and planning cannot dissuade all potential criminal activity, but there are proven design approaches which are effective in preventing and reducing crime. What types of design tactics do women advocate?

- Appropriate maintenance of vegetation around paths – through landscaping, caring for and pruning bushes – to better define the spaces between private and semi-private areas, and minimize blind stops provide pedestrians with good visibility.

- Improving and maintaining signage indicating public routes and discouraging access to private or unsupervised areas.

- Lighting, lighting, lighting! Well-lit streets and parks that promote optimum use throughout the year, but ensuring wildlife sensitivity by making sure that bats, insects and other wildlife are not negatively impacted by the artificial light.

- Seating areas with open views ensuring wholesome activities and behaviours.

- Bringing the inside to the outside and more social activity to the streets so that residents of all ages can experience more connectivity and, consequently, an improved sense of safety.

A female planner in a local council highlighted how often she reminds developers and architects on the need for more visual connection between the building and the streets, to provide opportunities for natural surveillance. Improving natural surveillance is a responsibility for all – planners, developers, architects and residents. Acting as a *Feedback loop* leverage point, it employs a systematic approach to monitoring and reducing the potential for street users to feel fear and criminals the opportunity to commit crimes. It also involves deepening the sense of place and extending the time women and girls can feel safe exploring and enjoying their communities.

Leverage Point 13 – Scheduling regular patrol walks by 'wardens who belong'

 Sense of safety is place specific. The vennels in Perth, the canal in Wester Hailes, the shopping mall in Drumchapel, are considered 'no-go areas' by many of the women in my research. In this context, they noted how the presence of police as a preventive measure plays an important role in maintaining their sense of safety, both in specific areas and in their communities in general. In fact, a quarter of the women I spoke with indicated the need for visible policing on their streets as a reassurance to make them feel safer. But not all 'police' are the same. More specifically, women referenced the need for community wardens who identified with the area.

> Pause for a moment. Think of a real no-go area in your neighbourhood. Imagine how much easier your life would be if you could travel swiftly through it at perilous times of the day? Visualise the same area being looked after by two community wardens who you recognise. Would it make any difference if you knew the area was looked after by them?

Generally speaking, community wardens can help with managing neighbourhood tensions, anti-social behaviour, fly tipping, graffiti, nuisance dogs and their owners, and littering. Many women argued for community wardens to be reinstated in their neighbourhoods as they strengthen the feeling that there is somebody around. The recurring presence of local wardens, acts as a self-reinforcing *Feedback loop* leverage point fostering an experience of reassurance for all urban residents, excepting those looking to cause mischief.

> During their daily foot patrols, the Community Safety Wardens traverse the cobbled streets of Alta de Lisboa, Baixa, Chiado, and Misericordia neighbourhoods of Lisbon.

These wardens have been selected through a participatory process led by the 'Grupo de Segurança' (Safety Group), constituted by residents, municipal police and local stakeholders who hold in-depth knowledge of the tensions and resources of their territories.[170] The first task of the Safety Group is to portray an ideal profile of a community warden prior to recruitment and training. Some of the positions are even assumed by residents, stepping into new roles! Being designated to specific territories over a long period of time enables wardens to gain recognition and trust from the community, as well as to develop interpersonal skills allowing them to deal with complex community challenges. The wardens' daily foot patrols, combined with monthly meetings by the Safety Group to discuss emerging issues, provide reassurance arising from a co-created and safer living environment.

Women I spoke to emphasised the distinction between the roles of community wardens and police officers. For them, while wardens are meant to guard, police enforce disciplinary power. Highlighting this distinction, a woman from Muirton in Perth confided: 'We have lost a community policewoman. A massive loss. Now we are "policed". Something that is done to us rather than a service for us'.

What if women designed their area's security systems? Firstly, they could advocate for a conceptual shift away from a police force to a police service. Both are about regulatory practices for safety; however, one relates to 'power over' while the other to 'knowledge with'. In this context, community wardens are there to promote community engagement and participation in safety matters, manage information exchange, and hold the balance between culturally diverse communities. A group of women from a Hindu community in Glasgow, for instance, suggested re-designating the countless wardens, whose primary responsibility is to issue parking penalties, to become community wardens, who could offer a safer environment for residents and non-residents alike to walk in freedom throughout their city: 'Like the park wardens of the old days'.

Presence and familiarity are key elements for this to work. It is important for the community to get to know their wardens and for the wardens to understand how their community operates. Scheduling regular patrols through public spaces by local wardens with clear job mandates to instil a sense of territorial accessibility and welcome amongst users can help people feel protected. Women may then develop a sense of trust in and for their city, and can set off on meandering routes where there will no longer be such a thing as a wrong turn.

Leverage Point 14 – Making practical cycle awareness training mandatory for drivers

 In a healthy active travel culture, motorists give way to cyclists and cyclists give way to pedestrians. In reality, complex power dynamics exist between the three road users who, depending on the circumstances, flip between playing the roles of victim and perpetrator. How to transform these tensions between street users was a hot topic amongst the women I interviewed who wished to cycle more but were often hesitant to do so. This leverage point speaks to the relationship between drivers and cyclists, and how to ensure a culture of greater mutual respect in developing a safe and effective road use to the benefit of both.

In the UK, women are less likely to use a bicycle as a means of transport than men, often because of concerns with journey quality and in particular to sharing the roads with motorised traffic.[171] Dutch cities are known for their cycling culture. Designed with networks of attractive and safe bicycle paths, they are developed to optimise journeys using a variety of transport modes, supported by an embodied code of rules, behaviours and fines. As a result, more women cycle in Dutch cities than men.[172] [173]

Cyclists in the Netherlands follow the rules of the road by adhering to traffic lights and signs, and not cycling on footpaths, pavements and motorways. If you don't follow the rules as a cyclist, you could be fined.[174] Using front and back lights on bicycles after dark is mandatory with a €60 fine for those who fail to comply. Additionally, a bicycle bell is compulsory and when passing someone, it is considered good practice to ring the bell – 'tring, tring!'. Stretching out your hand to signal the direction you are turning is also compulsory, with failure to do so running the risk of incurring a €40 fine. Furthermore, only two cyclists are permitted to ride side by side. Though bicycle fines are expensive, they help to ensure traffic safety. Other examples of fines include: €140 for holding a cell phone while cycling, €100 for crossing a red light, and €60 for driving in the bus lane.

In a country that has more bikes than people and where cycling is seen as a human right, drivers – who are also cyclists – tend to have a natural empathy for other road users. At road and cycle path junctions, cyclists are given priority, and you find many streets promoting *fietsstraat auto te gast*, meaning 'cars are guests'.[175]

The same cannot be said in cities where motor vehicles remain at the top of the travel hierarchy. Cycling for some women I interviewed in Scotland means challenging the traditional moral order of the road, where cars rule and cyclists are regarded as a nuisance. For car drivers, cyclists are often viewed with irritation when they fail to follow the same rules as cars, such as when they overtake queues of cars or travel well below the speed limit at a slower, leisurely and sometimes sociable pace. Groups of pro-cycling women argue for cyclists to hold the right to ride at the speed they want to and feel comfortable with, and denounced the general disregard of cyclists by drivers. For instance, the group 'InfraSisters' campaigns for a nighttime cycling infrastructure in Edinburgh that is safe and comfortable for women and girls.[176] Regular night rides put pressure on transport officials to design and deliver a safe, well-lit on-road infrastructure, and routes where cyclists are protected from traffic.

The charity 'Bike for Good' promotes a healthier cycling culture from its base in Glasgow's West End. The organisation refurbishes, repairs and teaches local groups how to cycle and how to maintain their bicycles.[177] They offer free bike rides for ethnic minority women to build their confidence and also promote bike festivals to encourage women to view themselves as cyclists, dismantling the idea that 'cycling is for XYZ, and often XYZ is a white man in lycra'. Amongst the variety of workshops they put on, they conduct a 2-day cycling awareness course for lorry drivers, to encourage them understand what it means to be a cyclist on roads dominated by motorised vehicles. The aim of the workshop is to educate drivers about their vehicles' potential blind spots and to make them more aware of the inherent risks to cyclists.

This leverage point is about changing the *Rules of the system* through incentives (to become a more empathic driver/cyclist and follow the rules) and constraints (or get fined). It emerged from conversations with experienced female cyclists who believe the tensions between drivers and cyclists could be reduced if all drivers attended a variation of the lorry drivers Practical Cycle Awareness Training (PCAT).[178] This could be made compulsory for all those who are applying for a driving licence or even associated with the annual MOT test. The PCAT allows drivers of large vehicles to step into the shoes of more vulnerable road users on bikes, on foot, in wheelchairs and mobility scooters, awakening drivers to a greater understanding of their needs and perspectives. Likewise, cyclists in cities should be able to pursue opportunities to improve their urban cycling skills. Women referred to the role of cycle companions who can encourage other women to cycle on their commute and on shorter rides, while obeying the rules of the road. By changing the rules of the system both drivers and cyclists can co-evolve in empathy, confidence and proficiency.

Further, making Practical Cycle Awareness Training mandatory for drivers of motor vehicles could help realise an empathic and friendly active travel culture, where cyclists and drivers co-exist safely and collaborate in the essential process of reversing the growth of road traffic and, in so doing, decarbonising transport systems.

Leverage Point 15 – Encouraging active travel as a way of life

 There are countless ways to define active travel. The Government of Ireland's definition, however, goes to the heart of the matter, defining active travel as 'travelling with a purpose using your own energy'.[179] Fundamentally, active travel is a mode of travel dependent on physical activity, like walking, cycling, wheeling and scooting used for commuting, leisure, and errands. Together, these represent multiple modes of travel used by women during their daily routines.

Historic neighbourhoods, designed prior to the advent of motorised vehicles, were intentionally compact, inter-connected, and provided convenient access to essential amenities within walking distance.[180] It is not by chance that mass motorisation and rapid expansion in car ownership coincided with the development of sprawling networks of neighbourhoods, stretching miles from city centres and requiring cars for commutes, shopping, and general access to services. Since the 1950s, fossil-fuel powered vehicles and their internal combustion engines have transformed modern society by providing independence and freedom of mobility, positioning motor vehicles at the top of travel hierarchy. But at a high price!

Car dependency is a complex topic which has been extensively debated. Some authors analyse it from an addiction to oil perspective,[181] [182] [183] some look at the impacts of car dependence – climate change, noise pollution, congestion and road safety [184] – while others investigate issues of identity, rank, attitudes, and norms.[185] Independent of these lines of thinking, the mindset that positions cars at the top of the travel hierarchy is changing in thought if not quite yet in practice, as we witness unprecedented aspirations to transform transport systems.

If women were to design cities, they would be planned for proximity rather than motorised mobility. The uniqueness of each neighbourhood would be interwoven by bike and pedestrian paths, along with well-networked, easy-to-navigate transportation systems. For women, walkable streets are vital for generating a sense of community. Several of my research participants shared a vision of streets for people not cars. While some argued for a city-wide approach, others talked about the pedestrianisation of parts of their neighbourhood and making their high streets no-through roads. Still, some emphasised the importance of negotiating with the urban and peri-urban land use pattern. An example illustrating this is the prevalence of car usage in Perth, Scotland, which can be attributed to the city's compact nature combined with dispersed housing. This particular circumstance highlights the need for active travel plans to consider the significant distances people have to travel to reach their destinations.

This leverage point is concerned with shifting mindset to acknowledge that roads belong to all users and not solely to cars. It challenges and transforms theories about zoned cities, with the presence of the car as the absolute point of reference. Thus, it supports the transition from car-centric cities to cities where traffic is evaporated, and people work with nature to create places that function at a speed conducive to living well. Women interviewed repeatedly referred to how the quality of primarily pedestrianised, wider pavements offering easy access for wheelchairs, mobility scooters and prams, influenced their travel choices. Aesthetically pleasing and well cared for pathways encourage people to drive less and walk more frequently, enjoying the aliveness of their local streets while frequenting local shops and cafés. The vision which emerges is one of the hopefulness of spring flowering, whispering that slow is beautiful and urban life must slow down to thrive.

Leverage Point 16 – Rethinking the bus fare system for 'trip-chaining', and redesigning buses for encumbered travel

  This leverage point combines *Parameters* with *Power to self-organise and evolve* transport systems, taking into consideration two specific travel patterns mostly unique to women. These are 'trip-chaining' – the need to make multiple stops for the purpose of transporting children, running errands, grocery shopping, and work-related activities[186] – and 'encumbered travel', which is understood as traveling with a child, an adult dependent or a heavy and difficult to manoeuvre item.[187]

There is long-standing research demonstrating that on average, women travel shorter distances and journey times compared to men.[188] [189] [190] While men who commute to an office workplace may travel on a simple journey involving a trip from home to office and then return, women tend to make multiple stops and pursue alternating modes of travel as they go about their daily lives. This is due to the gendered division of work and the varied roles women play during a single day involving employment, social life, household work, and caregiving. As women often pursue more sustainable travel patterns, adapting public transport to women's needs – and in particular empowering multi-modality – could lead to more sustainable transport patterns, enhance women's well-being and free more space for creative, social and 'me-time'.

Women believe that in order to encourage public transport use to and from, in and around their cities, it must be made more accessible, affordable and better connected. A recurrent theme was the establishment of an access-egress-transfer scheme[*], where women can switch modes of travel on the same ticket. For this to happen, more collaboration is needed between transport providers to develop a holistic gender-sensitive scheme. Indeed, several women advocated for a single ticket that could allow trip-chaining within a one-hour timeframe within a well-integrated network, making public transport more accessible for all. The Hopperfare in London – unlimited bus and tram journeys within a one-hour period – is a sound example.

For trends to become policies and schemes, there is a need to collect evidence at the local level on women's transport and mobility patterns, as well as preferences and time use statistics. Understanding better gender travel needs is a prerequisite for making the right decisions regarding sustainable urban and transport development; and identifying the appropriate levels of data disaggregation requires political will and intense methodological work.

Umeå in Sweden is known for bringing gender perspectives to the fore of urban planning, particularly in mobility and infrastructure decisions based on analysis of robust gender-disaggregated data.[191] The city has been keen to achieve a nuanced understanding of patterns in gender mobility and making statistics matter through enacting data-driven policies. For instance, research revealed that while commuting by bus to female-dominated workplaces such as the hospital was high, the patterns were different when it came to business and industrial districts. Inspired by a 2020 study commissioned by Sweden's Vinnova Innovation Agency which found that, if men travelled like women,

---

[*] A transportation strategy ensuring convenient access, smooth entry/exit, and seamless transfers between modes for an efficient and connected travel experience.

Sweden's emissions from passenger transport would decrease by nearly 20 percent,[192] a series of climate-smart choices for sustainable lifestyles were identified in Umeå. These included car-pooling, timetables aligned with working hours, and adding more bus stops to encourage men to change their behaviour by making the switch more appealing.

Besides trip-chaining, women are more likely than men to undertake encumbered travel. There is an ongoing debate on the division of space between buggies and wheelchairs on public transport. By law in UK, wheelchairs are given priority and parents are asked to fold down prams if the need arises or take the next bus.[193] For women in peri-urban areas such as in the suburbs of Perth in Scotland, this can mean waiting up to 40 minutes for the next bus. The solution, according to a mother from an ethnic minority background who travels encumbered daily, is to 'design buses with adaptable space for both'.

Leverage Point 17 — Designing 'fresh air routes' and low emissions zones from the perspective of women and infants

 Each walking interview was unique in its revelations. On one occasion in car-centred Perth, a participant led me on a route through the city centre, avoiding any interactions with motorised vehicles. We strolled through hidden passageways between buildings and quiet streets, alleyways and vennels, and along waterways and burns. This experience captured the essence of this leverage point recommending the establishment of fresh air routes to offset the fumes of congested and thunderous traffic.

The concept of 'fresh air routes' aligns with the increasing numbers of Low Emission Zones (LEZs) in operation, preparation or planning across 15 countries in Europe,[194] but advances the notion further. Whilst a Low Emission Zone eliminates the most polluting vehicles travelling in an area to reduce air pollution, they often fail to solve the problem alone – the affluent can still pay to allow their vehicles to enter! Fresh air routes go further and improve walkability, and the physical and mental health of infants and adults, by transforming disused pathways into breathable and enjoyable experiences, where the air is cleaner and exposure to fine particles reduced.

The High Line in New York is one such a 'fresh air route'.[195] Transformed from a disused railway line to a raised public park, this area on the West side of Manhattan was saved from demolition and repurposed by neighbourhood residents. The High Line opened in 2009 as a unique route where people experience nature, art and design free from the hustle and bustle of the congested streets below. It is now a continuous 1.45-mile-long greenway, connecting Gansevoort Street to 34th Street on Manhattan's West Side and home to 500+ species of trees, grasses, shrubs and wildflowers mingling with contemporary water features. The High Lane constitutes a fantastic example of community/public partnership where Friends of the High Line and NYC Department of Parks & Recreation pool resources and share a common vision. It also serves as an inspiration for cities to transform unused industrial infrastructures into health-promoting commuting routes.

It is generally understood that the faster the vehicle speed, the greater the exhaust emissions emitted. A study carried out at the University of Surrey suggests that children in prams are exposed to up to 60% more air pollution caused by road transport than adults.[196] This is due to the fact that children in prams are physically positioned between 0.55m and 0.85m above the ground, while vehicle exhaust pipes typically sit within 1m above road level. Additionally, this study revealed that the unhealthiest places for infants to be exposed to air pollution are at bus stops and traffic lights when they are waiting to cross a road. This was reaffirmed by several women living in housing estates, who expressed concern about the impact on their children's health from fumes emitted by fast-driving cars and motorcycles. Heavy traffic is also a reality in Portobello High Street, a densely populated shopping street in Edinburgh which cars speed through every day. Several women referred to the challenges they face in inhaling large quantities of fine particulates and street dust while waiting to crossroads, with too few designated crossings, and where vehicles approach from all directions.

Evolving a network of meandering fresh air routes connecting pockets of green and blues spaces as well as disused pathways in the neighbourhood is a *Power to add, change, evolve or self-organise* leverage point propelled by collaboration between neighbourhood parties with the potential for transformative outcomes. Advocating for such a vision, one woman stated that

'If there is a will there is a way', in referring to how urban planners, practitioners and residents could co-design an emerging network of fresh air routes where the effects of pollution are mitigated.

'Mums for Lungs' is a grassroots environmental group created to advocate for setting up 'school streets' around schools in UK.[197] They define a 'school street' as a temporary road closure for certain motor vehicles at school drop off and pick up times. Dedicating streets as 'school streets' reduces children's exposure to air pollution, improves air quality, increases road safety, and leads to greater use of active travel. School streets are becoming increasingly popular in the UK, with now more than 500 dedicated across London.[198] Hereford is planning to adopt the concept of 'school streets' by only allowing access to pedestrians, cyclists and permit-holding local drivers for 30-60 minute periods at the start and end of the school day.[199] 'Mums for Lungs' aspire to empower head teachers and parents to create as many traffic-free streets as schools across the UK.

Clean air is a human right. In cities pure air is rare, with often unacknowledged impacts on people's wellbeing. With air pollution globally responsible for 13 deaths per minute, the WHO reminds us that many of the drivers of pollution (i.e., vehicles using fossil fuel) are also sources of greenhouse gas emissions.[200] Time and again, I found women advocating for whole systems policies and environments. This leverage point can deliver for both health and climate. The women I interviewed want to transform their areas from being dominated by fast-moving highways into slow soulful pathways, that offer infants the possibility of travelling outdoors while breathing fresh air and taking in the sweeter scents of the earth, all of which can in turn enliven their existence. Every breath matters.

Leverage Point 18 – Promoting early interventions and co-creating values-based educational pathways

 Women and girls experience their neighbourhood through a set of physical, social and safety-related limiting factors that shapes their daily experience. Most of these hindrances remain invisible to men. This *Structure of Information flows* leverage point focuses on how to make the invisible, visible, and then how to transmute the visible into mutually respectful and enriching relationships. It does so by introducing discussions on the roles of women and men in embodying respect for each other as early as in primary school, through a values-based education.

Educating children about gender equality from an early age at home, in school and in the community is essential, as it happens at a critical stage in a child's learning about the world and their role in it. In this process, challenging traditional gender expectations and stereotypes paves the way for an equal world in the future. For example, rethinking the notions of 'strong' boys who should stifle their emotions and 'caring' girls whose role is to please others, might prevent adult stereotypes manifesting where women are supposed to nurture and avoid dominance, and men are expected to be proactive and avoid displaying any weakness. On this note, a woman in my research discussed the prescriptive components of gender stereotypes, stating: 'My child is 8 years old, and I already notice many unnecessary gender expectations at this young age'.

Several respondents believe that early interventions and capacity building in young adults could prevent acts of violence against women later in life. What sort of interventions are best? In the first instance, increasing safe, stable, and nurturing relationships between children and their parents and caregivers was one of the interventions identified by women as being effective. When this nurturing environment is absent, the community may be in a position to rally around and to adopt the Gandhian philosophy that 'it takes a village to raise a child'. One woman remarked on the importance of such an approach, emphasising that many children live in a state of constant distress. By introducing experiences of alternative realities, we can demonstrate that there are healthier and happier ways to live and thrive. Another referred to a community-based initiative called 'Dutch Safety House', which constitutes a space designed to provide a safe haven for children while in transit to and from school. Strong communities can play a vital role in creating the local conditions to help youth become engaged citizens, while preventing or reducing both juvenile delinquency and criminal victimisation.

Leeds, a medium-sized city in England, wanted to become recognised as a city that embodies kindness as a value through which citizens could grow, exchange and contribute to society. Inspired by Leeds Kindness Revolution and its associated festivals,[201] a group of women from Wester Hailes advocated for a culture of kindness extending to all children in the area, even those who can't find it at home. They hoped this sort of values-based community mobilisation effort could effectively enable children whose parents are hooked on drugs to break through the barriers they face, while developing an equitable gender perspective.

Pushing boundaries is a regular feature of the adolescent journey. This is the time when the community can serve as the buffer zone for young people to push against those boundaries – and hopefully not too far beyond their limits! Despite the youthful tendency to seek psychological distance from their carers, women's wisdom suggests this stage of life is more about connecting than correcting. Encouraging physical play or activity, investigating and exploring in nature and providing loosely curated community clubs, can provide space for boys and girls to become allies. In discussing the shared responsibility that comes with genders socialising and playing together, a woman reflected on the importance of awareness and vigilance. She pointed out that in situations where everyone is drinking and exploring, it is crucial for boys to be aware of potential dangers and be ready to step in and assist their female friends. While girls should be helped to identify the difference between a flirtation and a risky situation.

Urban youths are starved of opportunities to engage in rites of passage. In some traditional cultures, boys were sent into the wilderness to cope alone, while girls would be initiated by elder women. Today they compensate and create their own rites, sometimes through music and dance. This was the case with female teenagers from the periphery of São Paulo living in gang-dominated neighbourhoods. Despite hip hop beginning as a male-dominated cultural activity, *b-girls* and *funkeiras* use their music and dance to break the barriers of unequal power dynamics between girls and boys.[202] Their artistic production characterised by defiance and rebellion helps to reaffirm their female urban identities, creatively denouncing gender, race and economic inequalities.

Words are world making. Deconstructing gender stereotype begins with re-examining the language we use. While humanity is still referred to as 'mankind' within the main religious scriptures and practices; contemporary toponym* reveals streets named after men are far more numerous than those named after women; the collective 'we' is still referred to using the masculine form in the Latin languages; and AI utilises female voices (Amazon with Alexa, Google with Google

---

* A name given to a place or a geographic feature, such as a city, mountain, river, or street. It serves as a label or identifier for a specific location on the Earth's surface.

Assistant and Apple with Siri),[203] furthering the belief that women exist merely to help men get on with more important things...! Language needs deliberate attention, and radical – from Latin *radicalis, radix*, meaning 'relating to roots' – change.

Women are determined to deconstruct gender stereotypes from early in life onward, by leveraging information flows and re-thinking cultural patterns expressed in language, play roles, clothing, music and dance, and all assumptions that perpetuate notions of active men and passive women. There is a massive amount of work needed across the board to advance gender dynamics in society, fostering new perspectives of what constitutes femininity and masculinity in the 21st century.

Leverage Point 19 – Expanding the use of public space in the evenings by creating favourable bio-cultural-spatial conditions

 When designing to foster regenerative systems it is good practice to observe the interaction between territory and patterns of behaviour. Paying attention to traditions, triggering events and outside influences that bring forth one kind of behaviour rather than another, increases or decreases the liveability of a place.

The evening community stroll, *la passeggiata*, takes place each evening in the island of Ortigia, the historical heart of Syracuse, Sicily. A concerted collective movement without a *maestro*, people depart from their homes and stroll through the maze of ancient streets and alleyways converging and diverging from the magnificent baroque Piazza Duomo and Fonte Arethusa surrounded by papyrus, one of the most famous springs of the Greek world. The word *passeggiata* derives from the Italian verb *passeggiare*, which means to stroll.[204] The Italian evening ritual usually takes place before dinner. In Ortigia, people take a *passeggiata* roughly between 5 and 8 pm. On the weekends, entire families participate, and it can happen at any time during the day. The idea is that there is no rush and there is no final destination. People simply walk, slowly, and stop to catch up with one another along the way. The young flirt, the old socialise, the after-work relax – many dress up. It is an opportunity to see and be seen.

The relationship between women and urban spaces is intricate and dynamic. Women often choose their daily paths based on their mental maps. This relationship evolves as the sun sets leading to a shift to different evening mental maps. The once vibrant green and blue spaces frequented for exercise, play, and socialising during the day, transform into spaces influenced by external factors beyond their control as night approaches.

Feeling unsafe in the evening reduces women's freedom of movement and their ability to participate in cultural and night-time social and recreational activities. For decades, feminist geographers have examined what the triggers are for the *geographies of fear*[*] [205] [206] accumulated throughout a woman's lifetime and informing daily decisions. Those who feel 'edgy' in the evening attributed their sensitivity to two types of 'fear'. Some referred to anti-social behaviours associated with large groups ranging from street drinking, loudness and intimidation by the fires on the beach, or in public parks. However, one younger woman I interviewed insisted that 'those youth gatherings are not a threat to me because I used to be one of them. All they are doing is being young people having a good time'.

Others associated their anxiety with a bodily fear of crime, rape and femicide preventing their full participation in evening activities. Those women resented being housebound in the evenings, unable to enjoy night life. A woman I interviewed described the severity of the situation when witnessing an incident in Kelvingrove Park where one teenager got stabbed. She described the situation as frightening and reported it to the police.

This is a *Goal of the system* leverage point, concerned with articulating, standing up for and insisting on evening landscapes to be enjoyed by all. It is about women's acts of courage in converting gendered geographies of fear by reappropriating and reshaping their urban space. It is about the creation of the bio-cultural-spatial conditions needed to expand

---

[*] Spatial patterns and perceptions of fear and insecurity within a particular geographical context, influencing women's behaviours, experiences, and the use of space.

the use of public space in the evenings. And it is about understanding that no one action can accomplish this goal, but that a series of networked interventions may.

In terms of interventions, women spoke about the need for adequate and frequent maintenance of green spaces to avoid the impression that the place is not taken care of – as a way of enhancing their sense of safety while contributing to the aesthetic and physical quality of place. Designing and installing lighting systems can also improve safety perceptions. In addition, the importance of signage was emphasised, both in guiding individuals to public spaces within built-up areas and in creating a sense of arrival and transition to green spaces.

In terms of cultural interventions, women advocated for walking, cycling and running groups to nurture their confidence in the outdoors, in the city, and in the dark, while being sensible and assessing risky situations. Still, one woman suggested educating men about boundaries, while another proposed that when women are approached unsolicited on the street, they should counter with 'have I given you authorisation to speak with me?'.

In relation to the promotion of social events, one woman proposed the rebellious idea of men-free nights at Kelvingrove Park to allow women to enjoy the space in safety. 'This may upset men', she remarked, however when society suggests that women should prioritize their safety by staying indoors, she countered by suggesting that men should also stay indoors while women go out, as men are often the perpetrators of violence against women. Putting on men-free evenings in the park may open community conversations on gendered spatial patterns that need to be transformed, especially antisocial behaviours and harassment.

The word emancipation is derived from the Latin, e- 'out', *manus*- 'hand' and *capere*- 'to take', meaning freeing of an individual from the strong hand, or the legal authority to make her or his own way in the world.[207] This leverage point suggests that changing the goal of the system can transform places where women feel threatened to walk or linger during the evenings, to landscapes that foster women's emancipatory placemaking skills. And from there, we may just co-create the conditions for evening *passeggiatas* in all our neighbourhoods.

Leverage Point 20 – Co-developing sympathetic infrastructure enabling a sense of co-ownership and care

 Infrastructure sustains our urban world through networks of pipes, roads and wires, which typically only become visible when they break. This type of infrastructure also constitutes the underlying foundations of a neighbourhood, and as such provide opportunities for communities to take ownership of and change the places where they live. Urban infrastructures supporting such visions range from utility networks such as district heating systems, recycling and retrofitting schemes; to movement systems such as smart pavements, kerbs (curbs), traffic separators; as well as public spaces with toilets, seats and lighting.

A new concept of 'sympathetic infrastructure' emerged from the fieldwork, suggesting that building infrastructure with women in mind can have a ripple effect that can benefit other segments of society. Happy-to-chat benches, water fountains, repurposed band stands, smart and wildlife sensitive lighting, inclusive play parks, well-maintained and clean public toilets open year-round, were amongst the infrastructure upgrades most referred to by the women I spoke to, and all of which can be achieved if done with cooperation between the public, private and third sectors in conjunction with communities themselves.

More easily said than done. A distinctive characteristic of urban experience is the perpetual conflict over resources, development plans and infrastructure prioritisation. A woman stated that 'everything moves on resources', and when cuts to infrastructure expenditure happen, they fail to take into consideration women's needs. This is a *Power to add, change, evolve or self-organise system structure* leverage point applied to neighbourhood infrastructure. It calls for the establishment of locally adaptable, resource-conserving and collaborative designed approaches to infrastructure, coupled with self-assessment and evaluation conducted by the local communities themselves.

Women's everyday interactions with infrastructure are distinctive. They must contend with kerbs and uneven pavements when they go out with prams in their younger years, and later on when they become elderly and possibly wheelchair bound. Still there exist few ramps, and no automatic door-openers. In most cases, infrastructure is built to service the persona of a healthy white male in his forties. Donnella Meadows refers to how changing a physical structure is rarely simple after it is built, stating that 'the leverage point is in proper design in the first place'.[208] On how to humanize pavements and kerbs, a suggestion was proposed that traffic engineers should spend a week pushing a pram before drawing up plans for Low Emission Zones. Not that men do not push strollers; they are increasingly doing so (often with only one hand!), but women remain the majority who undertake such tasks. Such embodied experiences may provide engineers with the basis to design appropriate solutions, which they may not encounter if they are primarily working through policy red-tape and parameters.

Parks and other green infrastructure require regular care and improvement. Public toilets in green and blue spaces matter to everybody, regardless of their age, class, ethnic origin, gender, mental, or physical ability. However, they have particular importance to certain sections of our society, including older people, disabled people, women, families with young children, and visitors. What would it take for cities to acknowledge (and implement) the fact that access to clean and cared-for toilets is a human right that can promote everyone's dignity?

Portobello is embroiled in a sanitation crisis. In the area the lack of public toilets is a major concern. Visitors to the beach are left with no option but to find alternative places to relieve themselves, often resorting to using the back lanes. To illustrate the seriousness of the situation, two women I spoke with reported their front gardens being used as public toilets during the summer. On a more systems level, a group of women who are also swimmers, noticed that depending on rain, tide and rivers, there are days where the 'entire' city sewage comes to the sea.

Other interventions that could improve the experience of green places for women included wildlife sensitive lighting particularly in the dark months of the year. Another suggestion proposed by women was to consider benches, ideally with back and arm rests, as a social resource with options of facing one another and preferably avoiding cold stonework materials.

In terms of new infrastructure, women suggested that they wanted to make decisions to shape infrastructural measures that could lead to a more sustainable world. For instance, several commented on their experiences of electric vehicle charging point locations, with one woman stating: 'It is very likely that the whole charge point infrastructure system is decided by men in a room around a table'. This is reflected in charging points often being located in isolated, dimly lit corners of car parks, making women hesitant to sit alone while their cars are being charged.

Another low carbon lifestyle suggestion is to re-introduce collective washing lines to dry clothes in local green spaces. One of the women remembered the practice of her grandmother drying clothes in South Inch, by the Tay in Perth, overlooked from a short distance by an amphitheatre of hills. This is the reality of many Mediterranean countries – while Europeans have clothes washers in their homes, many do not have dryers. Instead, clothes lines or drying racks are part of the urban landscape. It doesn't matter if it is sub-zero weather clothes can still freeze-dry!

SDG 11 recognises the need for critical urban infrastructure to be low-emission, resource-efficient and resilient. A sympathetic approach to infrastructure can help evolve existing infrastructure through more deeply considering the needs and opinions of half of the human population. Only then can our imagined ideal of highly pedestrianised neighbourhoods with washing whipping in the wind, illuminated charge points for electric vehicles, abundant clean toilets, wildlife sensitive lighting, water fountains, social benches - all promoting an ethos of co-ownership and care - become more fully realised.

Leverage Point 21 – Maximising use of available local resources in urban interventions

 In nature there is no waste. This leverage point is about maximising the use (or closing the loop, when possible) of urban material and resources to support the regenerative capacity of neighbourhoods, through localised consumption and re-use and recovery of materials that are commonly wasted during urban upgrading.

Speaking about the disease of 'affluence' and all its associated discontents, US writer Wendel Berry defines consumerism as a state of helpless dependence on external things, services, ideas, and motives, leading to a disconnection from the earth and the ability to provide for ourselves.[209] For many, prosperity is defined as 'having more', a factor which drives consumption trends and the use and abuse of natural resources at never before seen levels. In fact, global resource consumption has risen significantly, reaching 100 billion tonnes per year in 2022, a substantial increase from the six billion tonnes recorded in 1990. This is accompanied by a corresponding amount of waste, with approximately 90 billion tonnes being discarded.[210] Per capita levels of resource consumption are at their highest level in human history.[211]

What role can women play in redressing these trends in cities? While SDG 11.6 argues that part of the solution is in waste management, we must go deeper and revisit consumption and production patterns. To begin with, women can mobilise their purchasing power to localise their economic systems. Whilst in the Global North women have a responsibility for reducing overconsumption and avoiding overuse of natural resources and material, those in the Global South are also key to shifting production processes and reducing waste production.

More and more women are becoming aware of the impacts on the environment that occur along product and service supply chains, as well as on the lives of those who produce the main products they use – but there is still a long way to go. Those I walked with during my research admitted the constraints they faced in reducing their consumption. For them, the challenge is how to promote a shift from a society of over-consumption of products and services to one based on well-being, belonging and sustainable living, where waste is minimised and re-use comes first.

The other side of waste management is a simple but powerful notion: maximising the use of local resources more productively saves money and can be better for the environment. In this context, women I spoke with indicated an interest in doing more with less – in particular, utilising local labour and materials to reduce their reliance on fossil-fuel based products and long supply chains. Indeed, they shared their emotional connection to hand-crafted objects and the local environments where they are sourced, and their satisfaction when they restore, patch or mend their own possessions.

A dynamic group of women volunteers I encountered brought life and art to a neglected community square located in a *gushet** close to Kelvin Park, Glasgow. Beautiful mosaics made from recycled tiles and glass embedded in the ground depict constellations, letters of the alphabet and some of the birds, animals and insects found in the garden. A volunteer mentioned that although their group is active, they believe in shared responsibility rather than placing the burden of solving everything on women. The same group was able to successfully fundraise to reinstate a historic wrought-iron entrance gate to the park, which had lain in storage for 30 years.[212] Built in 1897

---

* In the Scottish context, it refers to a small triangular or wedge-shaped piece of land, typically found at the junction of two roads or streets.

to commemorate Queen Victoria's 60-year reign, the gates were taken down by the council when their condition deteriorated. Expert repairs to the damaged intricate metal detail, reconstruction of sandstone columns and recreation of the glass lanterns from the photographs of the past, all required crafts(wo)manship. Such artisanal work can re-ignite our appreciation of urban installations that are handmade, slow-made and well-made.

When social enterprise 'Bridge 8 Hub' was established on the outskirts of Wester Hailes in Edinburgh, a canal clean-up took place over a huge area, with over 100 residents and community groups and businesses participating.[213] Over 200 bags of litter were collected between Hailes Quarry Park and the bypass, where trollies, bikes, tyres, and bottles had accumulated. Today, this space has welcomed a canal-based outdoor activity hub and also a community garden. A collective of women managing the herbal gardens are re-using pallets for plant beds, tables and seats. Garden tools are kept in re-used shipping containers, discarded car tyres function as insulated herb beds and old plastic drink cups and yogurt pots serve as plant pots.

At the heart of this leverage point is a celebration of community engagement in finding ways to meet local needs using local resources. In such a way, local materials are re-used, re-purposed and crafts(wo)manship rekindled for more regenerative environments.

Leverage Point 22 – Practising a culture of deep listening in the design and development of local plans

 What is the difference between community engagement and community mobilisation? Imagine a social field pregnant with bio-cultural-spatial potential that is yet to be realised. Engagement and mobilisation are two different lines of work needed to manifest this potential.

Mobilising implies a force stimulating and bringing people together for action. Local issues tend to rapidly mobilise the collective will and stimulate people to act, while policies can also mobilise people to respond. Between stimulus and response there is a space, and in that space community has the freedom to choose its response. Rooted in a long tradition of socio-spatial activism and facing a continuous flow of withdrawal of services, some women in Wester Hailes believed that: 'You need a big issue to mobilise people and right now, I am not sure people have a big enough issue that they all share to make them all want to come out and fight for that'.

From a classical mechanics perspective, mobilising can be seen as a centrifugal force originating from an issue and expanding outward to realise the higher potential of a place. By contrast, engagement can be seen as relational and centripetal reflecting what Newton described as 'a force by which bodies are drawn or impelled',[214] that attracts and holds the interest of community members to build an ever-expanding circle of participation and support.

Regarding engagement in Wester Hailes, one woman acknowledged the presence of a dedicated and active core group. One of its roles is to reach out to those who do not participate in community activities and to get them involved. This line of conversation prompted a deeper reflection on who includes who. For instance, a participant of Bangladeshi origin doesn't feel part of the community, a sentiment also expressed by a Syrian resident whose only interaction with the community occurs once a week when she collects food outside one of the agencies. The formation of a community welcoming group to support wider engagement of new residents was seen as a way to offset the social isolation of minority groups.

Depending on the circumstances, sometimes people refer to mobilisation as engagement and vice-versa. For both mobilisation and engagement to work, however, the women I spoke with identified deep listening as a quintessential requirement. Practising a culture of deep listening is a self-reinforcing *Feedback loop* leverage point, articulated by several women who believed generative listening fuels community-led initiatives and a spirit of entrepreneurship (centrifugal force), whilst also nurturing respect amongst stakeholders (centripetal force).

In this context, women in Wester Hailes (WH) questioned the depth of listening of periodic, tokenistic (and participatory) consultations on both master and local plans, coordinated by the political elite and architectural experts of the day. For several, WH is not a geographical entity that needs to undergo another cycle of upgrading to continue to exist, nor a problem to be solved. It is the centre of their universe, from where the construction of their identities is constantly reinforced. Women proudly referred to their (her/his)story of social activism, for instance, when creating the Harbour for women to take refuge in the 1970s. Time and again within possibilities and imagination, they have filled the gaps in the welfare state bludgeoned by years of austerity. Feeling reticent from decades of 'regeneration from above', the contemporary multicultural community feels the 'push and pull' between what is policy and what in effect are truly local plans. Now they want to create a

> women's hub to enliven the fading shopping area as a space
> to promote the entrepreneurial spirit of 'mums in business',
> and in turn create a culture of deep listening and
> transformative community-led projects.

Deep listening should be the bedrock of work undertaken by urban planners, officials and practitioners. Research from the European Commission Directorate-General for Environment illustrates the importance of comprehensive communication and consultation strategies with stakeholders from the outset and throughout the implementation of an active travel policy or project.[215] Several participants from the five areas researched, expressed having a similar experience of urban interventions being carried out without true democratic consultation – 'the Council does not engage', and when they do so it seems that 'it is nibbling around the edges' – resulting in scepticism about the Council, the politics, and the way that consultations are carried out. Furthermore, participants referred to a lack of clarity during 'jargony' digital consultations, particularly when utilising terms related to low-carbon living.

So how best to leverage deep listening in consultations that reflect the aspirations of the community? Women referred to creating conditions for generative listening to be practised between those shaping policies and interventions, and those who stand as 'beneficiaries'. Author, Meg Wheatley, discusses conversation as a means by which human beings have always thought new thoughts into being, creating a space of freedom for those who think differently.[216] Generative listening thus acts as a dynamic process of co-evolving ideas within a thematic area, engaging (centripetal) and mobilising (centrifugal) forms of thought and action, and resulting in complex levels of representation.

Take active travel as an example. There is recognition that some active travel and traffic reduction measures are contentious, requiring rigorous and careful consultation so that the diversity of views of the community are fairly reflected. Here the suggestion is to foster generative consultations that acknowledge multiple perspectives with a clear and realistic timeline, so people have the time to prepare and contribute to the processes. By going beyond tokenistic consultations, this process should be based upon a free, unbiased flow of information back and forth between women, community and active travel leaders as a means of nurturing a sense of equity in which everybody's voice is valued through genuinely democratic consultations.

A communicative turn in urban planning took place in the 90s. Since then, co-design, *charrettes** and consensus building processes have become buzzwords and events for reaffirming that knowledge is socially constructed (not only by experts and scientists). Women as half the population still do not feel represented in the policy and interventions originating from this era – more needs to be done. A culture of deep listening can create the crucible for generative ideas to emerge at the edges between the tacit knowledge of community members rooted in everyday experiences and the expert knowledge of technically-minded officials. Time to silence our preconceived ideas and truly listen.

---

* A collaborative design workshop involving stakeholders, such as architects, planners, community members, and other relevant parties to generate ideas and solutions for a specific project or problem.

Leverage Point 23 – Fostering regenerative tourism that enhances the bio-cultural-spatial uniqueness of place

 Regenerative tourism, a new concept that includes and transcends responsible and eco-tourism, has its roots in regenerative development and design theory.[217] It is about bringing in more life and leaving the places we visit in better condition than we found them. Anna Pollock, a regenerative researcher serving the international tourism sector, speaks about conscious travel as a regenerative approach to tourism development, ensuring all elements of the system flourish – guests, employees, businesses, and places.[218] Examples include local communities conserving pristine rainforest with eco-lodges or restoring biodiversity by stopping livestock grazing and reintroducing wild animals. But how best to apply this concept in urban settings?

Women living in the coastal community of Portobello in Edinburgh, which attracts an increasing influx of visitors, spoke about the threat of climate change leading to the urgency for lifestyle and behavioural change amongst residents and day visitors. As one woman expressed: 'We are a coastal community, and we are not bringing everybody with us, but we have to do it, because there is an urgency spelled clearly by science'.

Despite feeling coastal, Portobello is geographically locked between the sea on one side and the hills of Arthur's Seat on the other. Within this setting, a range of diverse habitats is easily accessible. From a regenerative perspective, 'abstaining from damaging' the area between the hills and sea is not enough. Beyond contributing to the local economy, visitors ought to leave behind a beneficial impact in the area. When asked what is it that they want other people to experience when visiting their area, the women I spoke with hoped for a wide range of methods supporting a conscious approach to urban tourism. These included opportunities for photography, storytelling, poetry, art, adventurous treks, and facilitated observation walks.

Place identification supports place-protective behaviours. Tourism is embedded in human-place interaction which are transient in nature. How do we awaken in visitors a protective/regenerative attitude towards the unique multi-layered network of living systems that constitute an urban area? Women spoke about the importance of identifying with the sea, the shore, and more-than-human inhabitants of Portobello, which could result in deeper respect and care developing by visitors for the local environment.

Fostering the concept of regenerative tourism is an *Information flows* leverage point. Sharing ideas and examples of how regenerative tourism enhances the bio-cultural-spatial uniqueness of place can inspire both hosts and visitors to adopt new behaviours. Anna Pollock advocates for developing the capacity of communities to understand and enact their roles as stewards within their environments.[219]

Findhorn, founded in 1962, is a pioneering eco-settlement located in the Northeast of Scotland. It continues to play a leading role as a research and development centre for low-carbon lifestyles, pursued through a complex melange of dream and vision, dance and chant, technology and spirit, investigation and design, reflection and action, death and renewal.

Six decades have passed since the community's founders parked their caravan in what later became known the 'Original Garden', sowing the initial seed for what has grown into an international centre of education hosting thousands from around the world. Today, the Findhorn ecovillage attracts over 10,000 day visitors a year who come to explore the prototyped solutions to the regenerative design challenge of our times in the areas of food production, renewable energy systems, ecological building, biodiversity remediation, circular economy and carbon footprint reductions; and most significantly, operating at the interface between the complex ecological and social systems and the interior dimensions of human consciousness.[220]

In Portobello, women believed that if visitors could experience a strong caring community which looks after its beaches, parks, woods and watercourses they might then gain a greater appreciation of the nature in their own community as well, and be willing to enact similar behaviour of care. Furthermore, more art on display, beauty and creativity expressed through cultural events, concerts, festivals, independent shops and open-air activities could also be promoted as a regenerative strategy for creating an inviting and inspirational image of the community, enhancing visitors' wellbeing experience and their willingness to return.

The role of community here is essential in curating activities and experiences that embody the beneficial harmony between human and natural systems. Communities become learning laboratories and regenerative destinations for those who are on the path to re-designing our human presence on Earth.

Leverage Point 24 – Adopting 20-minute neighbourhoods

 The vision of settlements designed and built to human scale is compelling: where living and working are reconciled and long trips to work become unnecessary, and where social and cultural activities, recreation and leisure are accessible for all.

Active travel, re-engagement with green spaces and the awakening of the spirit of community during the pandemic, provided growing evidence that the localisation of our lives could lead to substantial reductions in carbon footprints, addressing climate emergencies while deepening the sense of place. A key criterion for selecting the five areas of my research was neighbourhoods aspiring to embody some aspects of the emerging concept of 20-minute neighbourhoods.

The twin concepts of liveability and living locally in an area, where residents have access to all the services they need to live, learn and thrive within their immediate vicinity, has been named differently in different cities. In Paris, it is the 15-minute city;[221] in Melbourne 20 minute-neighbourhoods;[222] and in Portland, USA, 'healthy connected neighbourhoods'.[223]

The Melbourne Plan 2017-2050 is rooted in research that shows that 800 metres is the maximum distance people are willing to walk to meet their daily needs locally.[224] It has been estimated that walking 800 metres takes 10 minutes, and a 1,600 metres walk takes 20 minutes.[225] [226] Daily needs may include buying the basic necessities, accessing local health facilities and services, schools, and meeting friends at gathering places within a 20-minute return journey, using safe walking and cycling routes and local transport options. Estimates in Melbourne referred to daily reductions of travel by nine million passenger kilometres, which would lead to a decline in greenhouse gas emissions of more than 370,000 tonnes each day if 20-minute neighbourhoods existed across Melbourne.[227] In addition to significant reductions in greenhouse gas emissions, pollution and savings in infrastructure investments, additional benefits of improved health, reduction in household travel costs, better sense of place, and the encouragement of vibrant and safe neighbourhoods were the backbones of the Melbourne Plan.[228]

A key strategy to achieve substantial reductions of carbon emissions in the Portland Climate Action Plan is the idea of 'healthy connected neighbourhoods', supporting the health and well-being of residents and the vitality of local businesses. The 2015 Plan set an objective for vibrant neighbourhoods to be created across the city by 2030 in which 80% of Portland residents of all ages and abilities can easily walk or cycle to grocery stores, schools, libraries, parks, and gathering places within 20 minutes. The plan calls for reducing vehicle miles travelled per person in Portland from 17 miles per day in 2013 to 12 miles per day in 2030, and 6 miles per day in 2050.[229]

Called 'ville du quart d'heure', the concept of the '15-minute city' has become a central element in Mayor Anne Hidalgo's approach to improve the air pollution, liveability and climate resilience of Paris.[230] This concept, initially proposed in 2016, was co-created by Carlos Moreno, a Sorbonne academic and special advisor to the Mayor of Paris. Moreno draws inspiration from the notion of chrono-urbanism* which considers cities in relation to time, proximity, and the daily and seasonal rhythms of life, suggesting minimal travel among home, offices, restaurants, parks, hospitals and cultural venues.[231]

---

* A concept that emphasises the impact of time on daily routines, movement patterns, spatial organisation, and urban design, arguing that by optimising the use of time and reducing unnecessary commuting, cities can enhance the quality of life for their residents.

The 20-minute neighbourhood concept can be seen as a *Mindset* leverage point shaped by a collective awareness of shared responsibility for desirable urban futures. But who is to lead this persuasive urban planning trend that may save tonnes of carbon emissions, encourage healthy travel, promote natural surveillance, reverse the decline in local high streets and economies, and deepen the sense of community?

There has been a sustained attempt by local authorities to turn Scottish neighbourhoods into net-zero localised experiences of 20-minute neighbourhoods.[232] However, women believe participation by residents in 20-minute neighbourhood plans is essential for the redistribution of political power in favour of voices that are rarely heard – and may constitute an antidote to the grand and often unfulfilled expert-led regeneration and master plans of the past.

The vision of the 20-minute neighbourhood as a low traffic environment, was sometimes articulated in tandem with the localisation of the economy – as described by one of the women I spoke with: 'I like to buy my fish and vegetables locally. If you have no local shops to make community, you go to bigger shops by car'. This means building human-scale business ventures, encouraging more local jobs and prosperity, and less travel, packaging and waste. It also means promoting a slower pace of life: what the economist and film maker, Helena Norberg Hodge, calls building the 'economics of happiness'[233] that transforms the distancing and anonymity imposed by the global economy.

Yorkhill & Kelvingrove is a stimulating embodiment of the 20-minute concept, past and present. A nurse who migrated from Southeast Asia and settled in Yorkhill in the 1970s remarked on how 'handy' it was to live in the vicinity of the hospital. Indeed, the lifestyle she described closely resembles the contemporary notion of a 20-minute neighbourhood:

> *'People remember here as being the first migrant area. Everything we needed was within easy reach – grocery shops, schools, university, and hospitals – with the added convenience of Indian and ethnic minority stores. The temple, the Museum, the garden, the library were all close by. Sauchiehall Street was very famous. Not only did the area house the Sick Kids Hospital. but also the Queen Mother maternity, where mothers and babies were closely connected, often referred to as the 'umbilical cord'.*

From a joinery operating in the service lanes for 50 years to various local businesses, including greengrocers, fishmongers, medical practices, gyms, and a park, Yorkhill & Kelvingrove embodies the concept of a 20-minute neighbourhood. It offers a range of facilities and amenities to the extent that some women don't even feel like they are in a city. Indeed, one woman described the concept of a 20-minutes neighbourhood as it applies to Yorkhill as a place where 'you can enjoy life without being rich'.

As a leverage point in the *Mental Model* category, it is clear that implementing 20-minute neighbourhoods cannot be done by policies or planners alone. Rather, women who have an animated knowledge of their surroundings can be the protagonists of the idea of urban proximity, where residents can more easily access local jobs, retail, health, education and cultural services within a short distance of their homes. Through living locally and embodying this spatial metaphor, women can redefine power dynamics while enacting an urbanism of proximity.

Leverage Point 25 – Co-creating transitional safeguarding public spaces for young women

 Young women growing up in cities develop skills for how to navigate a range of interactions with friends, acquaintances and strangers. Insecure landscapes and unsolicited interactions awaken them to a form of anticipatory alertness that may become a second skin as they transition to adulthood. It is estimated that by 2030, around 700 million girls will be living in urban environments.[234] The potentially unsettling transition from youth to adulthood often comes with increased time spent socialising outside the home, and greater independence from parents. As such, this is a time which requires unique and subtle safeguarding systems, as well as the provision of spaces not only designed to safeguard but also to prepare young women for their adult lives.

Rules create contexts, define boundaries and also degrees of freedom. This is a *Rules of the system* leverage point which emerged through conversations with women, mothers, social workers, and friends involved in varying capacities with adolescent girls. This leverage point aims to strike a delicate equilibrium between safeguarding and empowering young women, addressing the distinct developmental needs of those who have outgrown playgrounds but are not yet fully involved in adult women's social activities.

As a principle, all girls should have the right to move safely through their city; however, this is not always the case. In Drumchapel housing estate in Glasgow, young women want safe, equal access to the streets at all times of the day and night, advocating for the importance of adequate street lighting as a gender right, and suggesting 'banging pans' (making noise) to challenge the indifference of planners and city officials to their needs.

A health worker in Drumchapel believed girls are maturing earlier than boys. For her, this is due to the quality of school meals but also the impact of social media in motivating young girls to go to the gym for the purpose of looking good and losing fat. There is an ongoing discussion on how social media shapes and reconstructs hopes, fears and fantasies of what constitutes contemporary femininity. On this theme, a woman warned that girls today tend to flaunt their stunning appearance through fashion choices and makeup, influenced by TV, but it is crucial for men to understand that the so called 'flaunting' is not an invitation.

Women I spoke to proposed the co-creation of cultural-spatial safeguarding systems that support young woman to increase their self-confidence and develop their assertiveness. Safeguarding systems here takes into consideration adolescents' agency rather than their victimisation, and takes account of their alertness in assessing and managing potential risks during their upbringing in cities. A woman introduced the concept of 'safeguarding sanctuaries', where young women can get help without being judged by youth workers or trusted adults in their community due to their behaviours. When asked what these 'sanctuaries' would look like, women suggested the creation of 'cool places' or unspecialised outdoor home bases for young girls to play, to hang around in and to form their notions of the world. Such spaces could offer opportunities for them to explore meaningful topics such as consent, as well as to challenge idealised constructions of femininity. These could be seen as transitional safeguarding spaces co-designed between adolescents, youth workers, architects, and planners through sketching, creating physical prototypes or storyboards, and together 'designing out' features that may provoke their fear. The design process in itself could enhance their self-representation and self-determination within decision-making systems, and reaffirm their confidence in assuming their right to the city.

The creation of dedicated areas for young girls in open public spaces where girls can be girls and no longer feel at risk, are emerging in many cities around the world. From Umeå to Hanoi, Malmo to Yangon, urban policies and interventions that have long neglected young women's needs are evolving. As a result, spaces have been created where they can feel safe, accepted, unjudged, and most of all be themselves, and flourish.

Leverage Point 26 – Combining gender and nature-based approaches to transform urban environments

 While strolling with women through the streets of Perth, Edinburgh and Glasgow, some interviewees raised parallels between a culture of abuse experienced by women in cities and the tendency to dominate nature – as highlighted by ecofeminists of the 1970s.

The term 'ecofeminism' was coined by French civil rights feminist, Françoise d'Eaubonne, in her book *Le Féminisme ou la Mort,* where she argued that the domination of women and the degradation of the environment were consequences of the same worldview, informed by patriarchy and capitalism.[235] Thus, she called on women to lead an ecological revolution and establish new relationships between humanity and nature, as well as between women and men. As a strategy, d'Eaubonne proposed a practical experiment for simultaneously advancing both agendas – where women's equality is not achieved at the expense of worsening the environment, and neither are environmental improvements gained at the expense of women.

Fast forward 40 years and the tide may finally be turning, not only for the sake of women but also in our hopes for the planet. The strategy proposed here is to change the goals of the system in a joined-up approach where the regeneration of biodiversity and the redistribution of power between genders can be advanced simultaneously. With this mind, the first movement is to transform a deep-seated anthropocentric perspective into a more bio-centric, gender-sensitive approach that can deliver multiple wins.

As a philosophy within environmental ethics, anthropocentrism is broadly defined as a human-centred belief system that views nature as the means to achieve human ends and well-being. It positions humans as separate from and superior to nature, which is managed for the benefit and improvement of the human condition. Elisabeth Wilson, in her provocative work entitled *The Sphinx in the City: Urban Life, the Control of Disorder, and Women*, highlights men's tendency to bring order to the disquieting and ambiguous aspects of urban life; while women embrace this ambiguity and find power within it.[236]

Nature-based solutions are an emerging trend within a bio-centric worldview which are informing different disciplines, including urban planning. They offer a strategy to address the effects of human interference on nature, such as climate change, biodiversity loss, and water and food security challenges.[237]

Whilst there is great value in such a concept, before we combine both agendas to benefit women and nature, we need to be mindful of the pitfalls of taking authoritarian approaches to solving problems. As such, we should avoid engineering solutions out of the same mindset that has created the problems in first place. This includes practices that highly impact living systems in one area (for example, through mining and infrastructure development) which are 'offset'* by investment in modified systems elsewhere (also known as 'nature-false solutions').[238]

But how to combine both agendas in practice? Some participants expressed the intention of committing random acts of kindness and care, as a way of living fearlessly and overhauling the system of domination that orders and controls public spaces, and in particular green spaces. Women mentioned promoting a ban of glyphosate use to control weeds in urban parks; supporting wildflower literacy; and overall, encouraging cleanliness and fostering beauty in urban

---

* The practice of compensating for one's own negative environmental impact by supporting projects or activities that reduce or mitigate greenhouse gas emissions or other harmful effects.

environments. Some also challenged architects and planners who, they believe, through professional arrogance, promoted elitist blueprints at the expense of the people who used their modernist buildings and housing developments.

Nature-based interventions in cities can enhance resilience. For example, the Chinese concept of Sponge cities where green roofs, retention tanks and wetlands absorb storm water, strengthening the draining systems in a city.[239] Equally, gender-balanced perspectives are informing the transformation of urban environments, albeit too slowly. The timely combination of both agendas can be manifested in ecologically sensitive communities that are willing to let go of control over a world that we still have much to learn about.

Leverage Point 27 – Infusing beauty into cities' form and function

 Seeing the city through the eyes of women unveiled beauty in unexpected corners. A recurring question that guided their reflections was: Can functionality and beauty coexist? Beauty was often alluded to as a key quality to pursue in the design of contemporary cities. Women's perception of beauty in urban environments was synonymous with soulful and lively neighbourhoods, spontaneously thriving at the edge of being *chaordic**– demonstrated by simultaneous appreciations of wildness and cleanliness.

Infusing beauty into urban form and function is a *Goal of the system* leverage point, achieved through intentional design and random acts of creativity by women as urban agents of change. Artistic elements can serve as urban acupressure, marking spaces, inspiring, and inviting reflection, and stimulating thought. But, you might inquire, what sort of art? The women I spoke with mentioned landscape art and flowing water features. Sculptures of women with names and identities, rather than more of the same public art where individual men's names are enshrined in monuments and women are personified through virtues such as justice, modesty and wisdom, or remain anonymous.

Whimsical art like the murals on lamp posts created by street artist, Liz Onda, redefining the electricity pylons that light the island of Florianópolis in unexpected ways;[240] or yarn bombs in which knitted and crocheted items are attached to parts of the urban landscape.[241] In a similar way, a woman participating in

---

* A dynamic state that combines elements of both chaos and order, creating an environment where self-organisation and creative emergence can occur within a framework of structure and purpose.

my research was interested in transforming the transmission towers crossing the Portobello area into 'high-voltage art'.

Beauty was also associated with the awakening of the 'senses of place', engaging the whole palette of senses through gentle stimulation of colours, textures, shapes, shadows, sounds, and smells. A participant demonstrated how the smell of flowering bushes informed her choice of which pathway to take for her daily commute. Some women suggested creating aromatic gardens to serve those who cannot see flowers and herbs. One woman specifically highlighted the sensory experience of listening to birds and identifying the native trees that existed in the area before her modernist settlement was built.

Women highlighted the importance of ensuring the aesthetics of their built environments openly recognised and reflected the past, awakening memory and emotions. When discussing architecture, they emphasised the value of buildings being rooted to their cultural and bio-regional heritage, expressed through vernacular styles that incorporate materials, patterns, symmetries, and colours that are distinct to their environment.

> Recall something beautiful you have unexpectedly experienced in a city that evoked a sense of awe – a breath-taking sunset, the fragrance of a rose garden, new life emerging between the cracks of a wall, or another aesthetic encounter within the spatial world. Pause to re-experience that moment of beauty as you slowly breathe in and breathe out. Notice the feelings that arise within your body.

Beauty extends beyond the visual realm and can encompass the social fabric of a city, including the diversity of its people. The more inclusive a city, the more beautifully it expresses itself. Women again highlighted the social dimension of city design, arguing that nothing is more critical than an inclusive and accessible relationship between people and space. Indeed, as an active contribution to the beauty of the city, a group of women of Asian ethnicity expressed their willingness to volunteer 'in planting all types of flowers and roses', so that their green spaces can become a source of inspiration and beauty for all who reside in the area. For women, through designing out inequalities, cities become more attractive for everyone.

Leverage Point 28 – Reconnecting broken links

 The forerunners of the modernist movement informing the design of housing estates in the UK believed that in improving what they perceived as the function of architecture, appropriate socio-economic uplift would follow suit and subsequently a better world would emerge. This assumption, however, has been challenged over the decades, with suggestions that large-scale modernist projects have in fact contributed to more social segregation. This was reaffirmed by women from Wester Hailes and Drumchapel, who live within housing estates and neighbourhoods dominated by rigid straight lines, exposed engineered building materials and minimal ornamentation.

Walking through the Wester Hailes Plaza, a participant noticed how the community survived years of 'very poorly designed public spaces', reinforcing a sense of anonymity and disconnect amongst residents rather than uplifting them. According to her, the empty public space was devoid of colour – 'in this area all was grey' – and there were 'no places where to sit and have your lunch in the sun'. She viewed the most recent green and wider landscape improvements of the area as holding the potential to enliven outdoor socialising in the community. Another woman agreed, stating that by upgrading the social spaces and enhancing conditions for interaction, 'maybe you can change residents' behaviour'.

Women living and working in both areas amidst remnants of the functional architecture of the past, identified enormous potential for reconnecting the indoors and outdoors. Concerning Wester Hailes, a participant argued that 'there is a broken link' between inside and outside, with most of the community buildings such as the churches and social hubs having very poor visibility, meaning when you sit inside you cannot see outside. In this context, and particularly with those members of the community who suffer ill health, 'all they do is they go to these hubs, and they go back home', and consequently move 'from one inside to the next inside'. Such experiences can have cumulative health impacts and compound a lack of engagement with the 'outer' aspects of life.

To address this, a Drumchapel participant suggested the need to 'start from inside and look out'. This means carefully considering the outside spaces you see and can access from communal spaces. What do windows and doors look out on and how can people access such spaces if they are there? A women-led collective in Drumchapel dreams of taking over an abandoned Pavilion situated in a park alongside a tennis court area, to help reconnect the broken links between inside and out.

A great example of reconnecting broken links between inner and outer locations can be seen in the relationship between the Basílica de Santa Maria d'Alacant – the oldest active church in Alicante, Spain – and its Piazza Santa Maria.[242] Built in Valencian Gothic style between the 14th and 16th centuries over the remains of a mosque, on a Spring sunlit Saturday the church hosted several marriages from morning to late evening. During a rich experience of social observation, I noticed the Piazza's two small cafés providing informal refreshments and facilities for mingling guests and the expectant grooms who had arrived earlier. At times, departing guests mingled with the fresh faced, camera-ready new guests arriving for the next ceremony. Fundamentally, the Piazza was as vital as the Basilica for the performance of the wedding ceremonies. As the day drew to a close and the last bouquets were tossed, petals danced through the air over joyous celebration and revelry, highlighting the essential and integral link between the Piazza and the Church in the unfolding of the ceremonies.

This leverage point was particularly significant for women living in the sterile modernist abstraction of housing estates, where the outside realm can be threatening and challenging, often characterised by badly-lit streets and walkways, and windy, underutilised, lonely, and dangerous open spaces, empty of convivial sites for the community to gather. Thus, people move from indoors to indoors as quickly as possible. This *Power to add, change, evolve or self-organise* leverage point concerns changes to the physical infrastructure of existing buildings, which includes widening windows, relocating doors, providing reassuring and uplifting pathways between inside and outside, and installing covered outdoor structures of varying sizes to facilitate informal play, gatherings, and local cultural events in natural spaces, which together can reconnect the broken links between indoors and outdoors.

Leverage Point 29 – Promoting the use of electric bikes

Innovative ideas about the potential of cycling amongst women emerged during the walking interviews, with electric bicycles (e-bikes) being considered the future of micro-mobility. The notion of micro-mobility is evolving, yet there is a broad consensus that it encompasses bikes, e-bikes, electric scooters, and shared systems relating to all these devices.[243] A shift from ownership to use of e-bikes was viewed by many as a way forward. One participant stated, 'if I could simply hire an e-bike instead owning one', this could potentially result in a fairer distribution of opportunities to use e-bikes in urban areas.

Electric bikes can take us further while employing the same amount of leg power as regular cycling might.[244] Some women, however, were unsure how far they could travel on a single charge. The range depends on the type of e-bike used (light, fold-up, hybrid, e-cargo), the battery size and whether one cycles only using the pedal-assist mode or not. From the speed you travel to terrain type, the weight of the rider to wind conditions – all exert an influence on how far one can travel on an e-bike with a single charge. This is one of the reasons why women suggested e-bike schemes which offer short-term opportunities for them to ride in relaxed and pleasant ways, while experiment how far e-bikes can take. Based on this experience, they can then incorporate (or not) e-bikes into their daily routines.

To encourage wider micro-mobility usage among women, the locations of bike fleets is paramount. Dockless systems were seen as hazardous for the disabled, while cluttering over-stressed pavements. Several women suggested placing e-bike fleets at strategic connective locations between transport, commercial and amenity hubs. For instance, in Perth, a woman argued for positioning the free e-bikes at the train station and at the Inches – the city's main green space – a regular route taken by the women I interviewed. Another woman suggested displaying a map of commuter cycling routes, highlighting designated cycling lanes alongside docking stations to facilitate orientation and further adoption of e-bikes.

Along the same lines, one of the participants was interested in hiring a cargo e-bike to transport things. In Portobello, there are ongoing discussions about collectively storing cargo bikes in order to address the challenge of their size, and finding a compromise between bike storage and car parking. 'Porty Community Energy' offers community members the opportunity to hire a Nihola Trike and an Urban Arrow bike on a day loan for a minimal contribution, with the possibility of borrowing the e-bikes for free – with no questions asked.

Participants also expressed multiple reasons for hiring e-bikes: a women implied that she would be interested in hiring one for her children; while another proposed a recycling scheme 'as children grow up you give away the old bike and get the next one'. In addition, a mother and her two girls argued for scooters schemes which 'can help to get you from A to B much quicker than walking'. Increased access to free bikes, or free for the first 30-minutes, were perceived as ways of increasing cycling uptake amongst women.

On many occasions, the women I spoke with wanted to take up cycling as a mode of transport but were not prepared to make the investment under the present conditions. This, therefore, can be addressed through a *Rule of the system* leverage point in which women are provided with short-term opportunities to try new micro-mobility options without having to invest large sums of money. Examples of such systems already in place include the Vélib system in Paris,[245] the Donkey Republic app in Copenhagen,[246] and the EnCicla programme in Medelin[247] – all of which address the beyond privately owned model of e-bikes and incorporate the aspirations of women. Fundamentally, it is clear that strategically locating e-bike docking schemes and stations near key points of attraction in cities has the potential to rapidly expand women's use of e-bikes.

Leverage Point 30 – Refurbishing pavements to accommodate high heels

 In my experience, very few women truly enjoy wearing heels. However, many still do so for a great variety of reasons. This is a *Rule of the system* leverage point that connects the cultural-spatial aspects of urban planning, whereby urban infrastructure is adapted to suit the mobility needs of women, including enabling them to move comfortably in the shoes they wish to wear.

High heels place more pressure on the forefoot (front of the foot) rather than on the heel, thereby causing the body to adapt to being off-balance.[248] Wearing high heels on a regular basis can affect posture, the spine, hips, calf muscles, knees, ankles, and feet. Injuries caused by falling with high heels can range from minor sprains to more serious fractures requiring surgery, with more impactful injuries occurring when one falls to the ground or down some stairs. Thus, women suggested pavement adaptation to make high heel use more comfortable and less hazardous.

'Women Friendly Seoul' was introduced as a mosaic of 90 small projects developed by the Korean municipality in consultation with feminists, residents and experts in women's studies to eliminate 'the inconveniences, anxiety and discomfort that women in Seoul experience on a daily basis'.[249] Among the interventions, the programme supported jobless women to find work, promised 7,000 more women's public restrooms, expanded a women's taxi services, added more public day-care centres and... paved streets to make them more high-heel friendly. The story goes that women complained that their heels often got stuck in cracks on the pavement in front of the city hall. Aware of this, the municipality was the first to commit to

> resurfacing pavements with a 'slightly spongy material' that
> makes them easier to walk on with high heels.

Heels have been worn by both women and men throughout the
world for many centuries. The invention of heels in the 16th
century is attributed to Catherine de Médici of Paris, who used
heels because of her short stature and soon made them
fashionable among European aristocrats.[250]

Contemporary women do not only wear heels to look taller;
they also wear them for display, performance, attractiveness,
confidence, and urbanity. Heels are a controversial topic within
feminist debate. Despite all these considerations, many women
still continue to wear them!

According to University of North Carolina professor, Sreedhari
Desai, high heels are ubiquitous in the workplace and their use
is loaded with powerful cultural meanings, offering scholars 'a
keyhole...through which we can examine the broader issue of
how gender inequality is created or recreated and maintained
over time'.[251] In her research on how heels affect women's
careers, Desai found that women who wear flat heeled shoes
were perceived as being more capable and tended to receive
higher evaluations of their competency from both men and
women aged in their 20s through to their 50s. Wearing heels is
no longer taken as a signal that a woman's willingness to
endure physical discomfort justifies her position in the
workplace.

Walking in heels is a science that requires practice. Taking a
stroll in trainers could not be further removed from the
experience of spending a night in stilettos – where you must
pay great attention to your balancing act. Moreover, fit matters.
In Spain, every woman has a trusted *zapatero* – a shoe repairer
who can file the heels to suit. In Italy, women are expected to
wear heels on special occasions, such as to weddings,
christenings and burials. Women in Seoul and those who still

don their high heels in Europe, believe that pavements along critical routes must be adapted to soften the brusque song their heels sing – clack clack clack – as they make their way through the urban milieu in their daily lives.

Leverage Point 31: Delineating and flowing through cycling infrastructure

 A recent global study found that women spend as much time engaging in active travel as men.[252] When it comes specifically to walking, women in the UK already lead the way, with 58% of journeys in London completed wholly on foot being made by women.[253] Similarly in Glasgow, women tend to walk more than men – 84% of women compared to 80% of men.[254] It is interesting to note, however, women in the UK are significantly less inclined to cycle compared to men, primarily because their neighbourhoods lack protected infrastructure, which makes them feel unsafe and vulnerable.

As active travel trends globally, more gender-sensitive cycling infrastructure is needed. Encouraging cycling isn't enough, we also need to enable it. For instance, there is a need for freshen up facilities for women who don't want to arrive hot and sweaty after cycling to the office. In terms of appropriate lighting, in general, women cycle longer routes to avoid streets that don't feel well-lit. Additionally, they only invest in bicycles if they know there is safe storage at active travel hubs, like train stations – 'somewhere where I can leave my bike and be sure it will be there when I'm back' as a woman I spoke with put it.

What comes first: infrastructure or behaviour change? For Donella Meadows, shifting physical infrastructure is usually the slowest and most expensive type of change to make in a system.[255] Women repeatedly referred to the need to 'delineate and flow' through segregated cycle lanes, separating the cycle path from the road and footpaths. Physical separation from motor traffic may encourage more women to ride a bike through reducing motor vehicle interactions, something many women said they lacked confidence to do. Segregated lanes combined with well-lit streets (without disturbing residents or wildlife) were viewed as key investments in encouraging women to take up cycling.

Even if a protected cycleway is installed along every street or outside every house, getting started with cycling can be harder for some women than for others. A participant in the housing estate Drumchapel recounted: 'I fondly remember growing up in an area where you learnt to cycle on the road with minimal car use'. However, this was not the case for many residents, particularly those from an Asian background: 'I am a busy Mum with 6 children I don't have the time to learn how to ride bikes'. Non-cycling participants indicated that they would be more inclined to cycle if it felt safer. This attitude reflects the findings of a UK-wide study that found that while 68% of women believe their city would be a better place if more people travelled by bike: 73% almost never do so – primarily because of safety fears.[256]

Copenhagen is the best example of the 'delineate and flow' concept. Indeed, in urban planning the term 'Copenhagenization' is sometimes employed to describe the implementation of segregated pedestrian and cycle routes, contributing to a system in Copenhagen of fully connected and stimulating bike lanes covering 385 kilometres, in almost every street of the city.[257] During commuting hours, when more than 60% of Danes cycle to work or school, you will witness streams of cyclists in free flow.[258] While at rush hour, I experienced a true thrill in joining the fast flowing cycle traffic along the unidirectional bike lanes.

Copenhagen is also unique for its cargo bikes, used to transport parcels, dogs, house plants, and even furniture but mostly for carrying children. In particular, it is known for the Christiania brand, which was developed in the famous counter-cultural Christiania neighbourhood by a resident who was inspired to move the bodywork of a bike trailer to the front of a tricycle, therefore allowing permanent contact between children and cyclist and making the transportation of children safer and more pleasant.[259] Compared with many cities, Copenhagen is relatively compact and flat. This, combined with wide lanes designed and built to accommodate cargo bikes so that parents and carers can transport their children, results in 26% of families owning a cargo bike.

In terms of policy and investment in cycling infrastructure, two additional *Material flows* leverage points were highlighted by women in my research. Firstly, ensuring segregated lanes reach to the heart of neighbourhoods instead of focusing on and investing in largely hard-to-reach national routes. And, when routes stretch to residential areas, lanes need to be free from parking opportunities, with clear road markings such as bollards or kerbs. Those in my Scottish case studies who dare to cycle along dark, unlit pathways during the winter months, spoke about the significance of improvements in lighting combined with vegetation maintenance and shortening of distance between cat's eyes. This has been the goal of a campaign led by an Edinburgh collective 'Light up the Night', in which cyclists take to the streets with their bicycles decorated in lights to campaign for safer cycle paths appropriately illuminated in the dark.[260]

Women believe that cycling can be a safe, convenient and enjoyable mode of transportation for them if a network of simple, well-lit and connected infrastructure is developed and implemented. These requirements need to be supported by transport policy and practice. If they are met – as they must be – women may move more freely by bike and less by car.

Leverage Point 32 – Purpose-building inter-generational housing

  People are living longer than ever, well beyond their age of retirement. This leverage point addresses ageing populations as a defining megatrend in our cities. Some have termed this demographic 'the Silver Generation'. According to UN DESA World Social Report 2023, globally a baby born in 2021 can expect to live on average almost 25 years longer than a new-born from 1950, reaching 71 years – with women outliving men by an average of five years.[261] The combination of improvements in health systems (with vaccines and antibiotics), lifestyles and food systems' productivity are considered the drivers of human longevity.

As the term suggests, megatrends occur on a large scale and unfold over an extended period of time. They are set in motion through incremental changes that take decades to display their true magnitude. They are factual and often backed by verifiable data involving a complex combination of factors within and between social, political, economic, technological, and environmental systems. They can also be influenced by significant or surprise extreme events.

Before the Covid-19 pandemic, people who had already survived to age 65 could expect to live on average an additional 18 years worldwide. Contrary to prior decades, celebrating one's 80th birthday is now an expectation rather than an exception.[262] In 2020, data from Japan's Health, Labour and Welfare Ministry revealed that, in Japan, 1 in 1,500 people reach the age of 100 or older – and those who do are more than likely to be women.[263]

This leverage point combines *Rules of the system* with the *Structure of material flows*, and concerns intergenerational incentives combined with design decisions that address a growing aging population while preventing loneliness for older women. With this in mind, a woman participating in my research suggested positioning nurseries and schools next to old people's homes. Why do this? She argued that as soon as the school bell rings signalling the beginning of the summer holidays – just as everything is ripening – gardening plots in schools are abandoned and vegetables go to waste. If old people's homes were linked to schools, then school gardens could be better taken care of. Over the year, the elderly could also share their experiences through their involvement with the school garden and perhaps nurture children's sense of co-creation with nature, which may help to reduce disruptive behaviours during adolescence and the impetus to control nature during adulthood.

Such initiatives could draw inspiration from the German model of multigenerational houses (Mehrgenerationenhaus), where older people and children mix to the advantage of both. These intergenerational living arrangements recreate some of the extended family ties that Western societies have departed from over the last two centuries. Prototyped in 2006 in Salzgitter, these houses were intended to bring under the same roof groups that had previously operated in isolation from each other – childcare groups, youth centres, young mother's support groups, day care for older people, and citizen advice centres. By consolidating social services, a variety of demographic groups come together, connecting those starting in life and those completing their life's journey. Currently, there are over 500 multigenerational houses operating in Germany.[264]

Alicante is Spain has an aging population. A 2022 National Institute of Statistics (INE) report stated that 20.46% of the Alicante Province population is aged 65 and over with 2.8%

over 85 years old.[265] Early in the morning, Playa del Postiguet, a long, clean, sandy beach in urban Alicante becomes one the most popular meeting places for senior women. Here they can choose to participate in a wide offering of exercise classes, from yoga to salsa. Late in the afternoon, the Postiguet promenade transitions into a place for strolling, meeting friends, or gazing towards the Mediterranean horizon. This is the closest beach to the Edificio Municipal Plaza de América, one of the most innovative projects in the field of social architecture and purpose-built intergenerational housing.[266] The scheme combines housing for older people with lodgings for individuals under 35 on low income, who actively participate in the daily running of the building on a voluntary basis. For instance, every younger tenant looks after four senior tenants on her or his floor. Not only were the buildings designed with accessibility in mind to enable social interactions, but they also offer a well-conceived on-going programme of activities nurturing a sense of belonging and community living. These include a 'Back to Earth' component with vegetable gardening; 'From Culture to Information' activities linked to storytelling, videos, books, music and newspapers; 'Fiesta' events which gather the community for celebrations; 'Technology in your Hands' workshops introducing the older tenants to new technologies; and finally 'Good Neighbour' activities in which younger tenants help older residents with their domestic chores or perhaps accompany them to the doctor or pharmacy.[267] The social and functional architecture of Plaza de América in Alicante designed by two women architects, Carmen Pérez Molpeceres and Consuelo Argüelles Álvarez, is probably the most interesting example of intergenerational architecture in Spain, facilitating an enriching coexistence between younger residents and the silver generation.

When referring to potential scenarios of aging in cities, women reflected on the trend of living longer, aspiring to be free from cognitive or physical impairment while experiencing and contributing to rich intergenerational exchange and affection. One of my interviewees shared that she relied on two grandmothers as she grew up, and later they became dependent on her. This experience shaped her into a more caring person. She believes that all children should have such opportunities. Our increasing longevity is stretching the boundaries of life experience, unleashing a quiet cultural transformation, and challenging our resolve to support everyone in adding years to their lives and life to their years.

Leverage Point 33 – Co-designing places with (not only for) teenage girls

 A recent UK-based study by the organisation Making Spaces for Girls revealed how parks, play equipment and green spaces for teenagers are currently designed with the default male persona in mind.[268] The focus often centres on skate parks, BMX tracks and competitive sports facilities, leaving little provision for the specific needs and preferences of teenage girls.

This leverage point involves co-design, which emphasises designing *with* girls rather than just *for* them. To achieve this, we need to learn what makes today's teenage girls unique and the cultural forces shaping their experiences. Termed 'iGens' by social psychologist Jean M. Twenge,[269] this generation, also known as Gen Z, has been shaped by digital technologies, climate anxiety and pandemic lockdowns. While the association of this age group with iPhones may be limited to the Global North, it is undeniable that smartphones and social media have had a significant impact on the lives of teenage girls worldwide. It is worth noting that virtual connectivity can sometimes hinder real-world friendships and the ability of teenagers to fully engage with the world around them.

This leverage point indicates a growing need to co-design unspecialised outdoor spaces for teenage girls to hang out and to form their notions of the world, away from their screens. Co-design in this context invites teenage girls to input ideas into the spatial arrangements (alongside urban planners and architects), where they can connect with and nurture their rightful sense of belonging to green and public spaces. Specialists here are challenged to expand their generative listening, instead of prescribing spaces and curating activities that may not resonate with Gen Z. This is an *Information flow* leverage point whereby a new information loop is created through participatory means, leading to shifts in behaviours amongst both teens and designers.

Bredäng park, situated in a modernist suburban area of Stockholm of the same name, is a great example of urban intervention co-developed with teenage girls. Originally the site was dominated by a football pitch, used mainly for organised sports events for boys and men. Based on evidence that most of the Swedish youth do not engage enough in daily physical activity (a tendency particularly pressing amongst teenage girls), the landscape designers, Nivå Landskapsarkitektur, convened focus groups with teenage girls to discover what sort of structures would encourage them to use and do more in the park.[270] Through a series of workshops, the co-design group developed a design for mixed-use play-spaces aimed at stimulating spontaneous physical activity more broadly. A pergola and a stage with stepped seating contributes to a park's landscape, which can be used throughout the day and in all seasons. Well-lit and equipped with Bluetooth speakers, the park allows users to enjoy their own music, fostering a space for impromptu dance, play and free sports where teenage girls can spend time together.

Every generation of teens is shaped by the cultural, environmental and political forces of the day - and today's teenagers are no different. Gen Z is a generation concerned with global warming, inspired action and restoration of the planet. It is also a generation steeped in the virtual world and intensive screen-time. This leverage point is about co-designing urban spaces for girls that can foster their ecological connectivity, deepen their social connections and expand their spatial imagination.

8 | Bridging the Gender Gap in Urban Planning

'Spatial planning exists by the grace of good story-telling.'
~ Zef Hemel ~

My research involved listening to 274 women over a period of 6 months, and included walking interviews, each of which was unique in its revelations. All conversations were initiated with the kick-off question: 'what is unique about your neighbourhood?' From there, participants made all the decisions, including the route followed, the duration of the interview, the walking pace, and what they wanted to show and share. They were given control over the research process and invited to step into the role of experts of their area. Some women adapted the route to fit in with their everyday life, such as their daily walk in nature or to a Post Office, or even a school pick-up.

Participant insights were ultimately organised into 33 leverage points ranging from mental models to infrastructure upgrades, from feedback loops to redirecting material flows. Before we begin activating leverage points and turning them into policies and practices, we need to prepare for the journey by making one collective decision and awakening three awarenesses.

This decision is centred around choosing not to navigate our way using an old map to reach a new territory. Rather, it means that, despite the fact that cities have historically utilised a white, able-bodied, adult male person as reference for their spatial planning, we must let go of a zero-sum perspective where women's centrality to urban planning means other genders lose out.

The new map we are creating is one of co-evolving mutualism rooted in a desire for inclusivity, an embodiment of care, and an acknowledgment of complexity. Co-evolving mutualism here means engaging with and listening to all who have a stake in the system, in reflective and generative dialogue which encourages learning together.

I argue here for intentionally widening the urban planning expert-led horizons and seeking out people who have different (even opposing) perspectives from our own, identifying bewildering and bewitching lines of work for co-evolving cities that work much better for children, older people, all levels of ableness, and gender identities. Living successfully in a world of complex urban systems means working towards the good and liveability of the whole.

First Awareness – Transition is going to happen

We are grappling with the question of how we want our cities to perform for communities, wildlife and ecosystems. Will cities of the future become smart, efficient, green or just? Hundreds of scenarios for the cities of the future are projected by agenda holders, think-tanks, urbanists, climate scientists, geographers, futurists, economists, big data analysts, generating a plethora of urban frameworks including sustainable cities, eco-cities, green cities, smart cities, biophilic cities, soft cities, net-zero cities, climate-neutral cities, feminist cities, and more.

Transitions are inevitable. Either we design for them, or we become their victims. This book reaffirms the role of women in designing for urban transitions. We understand design as a collective process of envisioning, reflecting, conceiving, and imagining how to re-design our human presence on the planet, particularly in the urban environments. But what is the mindset that should inform this most fundamental design endeavour? This leads us to the second awareness, related to the direction of travel.

Second awareness – Redefining the direction of travel

Merely pursing sustainability is not enough. How can we sustainably bring back something that has been lost? Living systems and urban environments have become victim to our high consumption lifestyles and our linear, growth economies. By adopting a regenerative perspective, we purposively bring more life, vitality and viability to our urban environments – ensuring they can co-evolve with ecological systems over time.

By questioning the theory of change that guides 'sustainability' (making the problems less bad), we are able to let go of a problem-solving mindset. Instead, we adopt the notion of potential rooted in the bio-cultural-spatial uniqueness of place. Thus, the second awareness centres around focusing our collective gaze on what is strong, not on what is wrong. Furthermore, we build the regenerative case on what is local and unique. Through networks of proximity within connected neighbourhoods, people move from a transactional to a relational way of life, fostering a sense of collective motivation.

Third awareness – Elucidating women's roles

Intrinsic to my investigation was a desire to create space for women to elucidate the roles they were either already playing or were prepared to take in challenging and re-designing the forms and values encoded in a male-referenced urban environment. 'Elucidate' originates from the Latin term *lucidus*, which means lucid. *Lucidus*, in turn, comes from the verb *lucēre*, meaning to shine.[271] In this context, elucidating means shining a light on the roles women are prepared to step into (as subjects of urban realities) in order to make it easier to see and remedy their urban reality.

In general, women as regenerative designers were not interested in managing the entropy of failing systems and solving urban problems one at the time. Instead, cities were viewed as a vehicle for their emancipation, providing a range of new job opportunities for individual and particular groups of women. The specific role titles – free from reproducing gender stereotypes such as the caring role – speak for themselves. In sense of place, women identified the roles of Engaging New Neighbours, Nurturing Community, Spreading Kindness, Designing for Inclusiveness, Setting Agendas, and Dynamising the Edges. Roles related to green spaces included Growing Food Together, Promoting an Ethic of Care, Designing Nature Corridors, Educating Outdoors and Adventurously, Nature-based Health Carers, Volunteering for Wild Places, and Mobilising Resources.

For women, an active travel agenda can be advanced through the roles of Promoting Traffic Evaporation, Consulting End-Users, Promoting Comfortable Cycling, Advocating for Speed Limit, and Changing Travel Culture. Furthermore, in safety matters, the roles identified included Deconstructing Gender Stereotype, Facilitators of Non-Accusatory Conversations, Preparing to Stand-up, Networking for Safety, Providing the Eyes upon the Street, Educating Boys and Men, Reassuring

Women, Modelling Empathy and Consent, and Advocating for the Right to Entertainment.

If we cannot imagine the future we want to create we will never get there. Therefore, if we wake up in the morning within a city where women have taken all these fairly paid roles, how would it feel, look and function?

If women designed the city ...

If women designed cities, they could be greener and more sympathetic for nature. Green spaces could be more lively and colourful with a variety of flowers and extensive interconnected habitat patches dedicated to nurturing wildlife. In cities, biodiversity could be promoted through the installation of living walls, roof gardens and pocket parks; all connected to create green corridors for people to take pleasure in the fresh air, and for wildlife to move more freely about the city. Emphasis should be placed on planting fruit trees and in greening crossings and junctions, with shrubs and bushes used as screens and backgrounds that encourage birds. There could be food growing activities spread throughout the city with easier access to allotments; school gardens where children can learn about plants; and herbal planter boxes that could be harvested by everyone. Green spaces would have dedicated flower gardens that could be picked for home or for communal places of worship; and scented gardens to stimulate the senses of all individuals including the older and the disabled. There could also be opportunities for people to socialise with animals. Women could be encouraged to dry clothes in communal spaces and mums to exercise with their push chairs. Adventurous play parks integrated into the community could support children to push their boundaries and play together with their peers, parents and carers. In terms of infrastructure, wildlife sensitive lighting schemes could be installed, as well as picnic tables, ample recycling facilities, accessible toilets, and a balanced use of communal land between competitive sports and dedicated areas for young girls. In blue spaces, cities could take full advantage of coastal richness, admiring and respecting the diversity of marine species. Lastly, green spaces could offer an experience of flourishing environments, supporting a culture where those who care for parklands are well paid and volunteer workers are recognised, valued and empowered.

If women designed the city, there could be diverse outdoor and indoor socially-engaging spaces, cared for and managed by the community residents themselves. A new breath of life could re-purpose forgotten empty buildings, which could then be used to welcome new groups into the city, thereby enriching cultural diversity. A people-oriented city could reinforce local identities while nurturing a sense of equity and valuing everybody's voices in genuinely democratic consultations. Public spaces could then be designed to integrate different abilities and create conditions to encourage the mixing of all ages, from the young to the older. One such approach would be transgenerational homes available in every district. In parallel, nurseries could be built next to old people's homes and assisted care facilities. More communal living could be initiated, providing an alternative to people living alone and in isolation. There could be more focus on well-being and more opportunities for children and youth as they transition from sports to adventure to social enterprises. Fully accessible community activities, projects and opportunities could allow people to gather and belong without having to necessarily spend money. Alternatively, independent cafés and eat-ins could provide space for fostering neighbourly relations. There could be more art on display, beauty and creativity expressed through cultural events, concerts, festivals and open-air activities, widely promoted through public information boards. Additionally, a holistic model of healthcare and a women's clinic could provide services for women as they go through their life. Overall, people could experience a heightened sense of care for each other and for their city.

If women designed the city, safety could be more effectively prioritised. Emphasis could be given to natural surveillance, good interactive lighting and managing vegetation to provide comfort and wildlife benefits. Under such circumstances, circles of women responsible for neighbourhood watch and enforcing zero tolerance policies to counter violence against women could be established. Anti-misogyny laws could not only be acknowledged by all, but enacted and enforced, making clear that harassment is not accepted as banter. Community wardens with well-defined job roles could have a visible presence allowing all people to feel protected. Women could then develop trust in the city and feel empowered to take meandering routes where there would be no such a thing as a wrong turn. Monitored cameras could be installed in bus shelters, bicycle lockers and potential zones of likely incidents such as outside pubs. Furthermore, women could be better represented in urban design and planning decisions related to safety measures, which in turn could help optimise infrastructure investments to meet the safety needs of the entire population. Lastly, free self-defense classes could be made available to all those who wanted them.

If women designed the city, it would be easier for women to move around within the city because they would have contributed to its design and ensured its functionality. Walking and cycling could be the preferred travel options with roads being reclaimed for people. Instead of pedestrian and cyclists moving around cars, cars could have designated roads where they are allowed to travel. There could also be more time to cross at the lights and less car dominance. Indeed, cars would be viewed as guests. Initiating these steps would allow for the city to move at a slower pace; streets would be less busy, cars slower – but compassionate guidelines could be available for those who need access by car. More availability of EV charge points in illuminated spaces and less dependency on fossil fuels, with low emission zones spreading throughout the city, could become the norm. Adding adequate park and ride space outside neighbourhoods could be connected by small electric buses on demand. Routes could be well-lit and involve cyclists in the design. There would be affordable rental schemes of e-bikes and cargo bikes for carrying shopping, DIY and children. Largely pedestrianised, wider pavements could offer easy access to wheelchairs, mobility scooters and prams. Pathways could be aesthetically pleasing and beautified, encouraging people to drive less to access their daily needs such as local shops, markets, small supermarkets, fishmongers, and cafés.

Affordable (or free for those in need) transport systems could support trip-chaining and encumbered travel, linked through beautified interchange hubs of easy and safe access. Women could ensure bus routes exist connecting to their places of gathering and worship.

Spatially, things could be brought closer together, enabling women to transition more seamlessly between roles such as employee, mother and daughter, without extensive travel. This could involve establishing local hubs for workspace rather than relying heavily on a centralised city centre. Architecture could be more interesting, reflecting different characters of design and the needs of people, rather than boring, monotone and ordinary structures. Buildings would likely be lower rather than higher, quite practical, and take more notice of how people interact with the space from the perspective of the young, old and disabled. New houses could be equipped with solar panels and high quality and sustainable insulation. Tenements could offer space for gatherings, and children would be cared for and mindfully watched by people residing in the houses surrounding their streets. Simple things like pavements designed with smooth surfaces to accommodate strollers and wheelchairs, ensuring easier mobility, would be standard.

If women designed the city, straight line mentality and rigidity would most likely be greatly reduced. Cities could become places where people can meander, with opportunities to discover something new and unexpected, and where one can also walk and feel safe moving along direct pathways. Squares and boulevards would be well lit, benches carefully maintained and inviting, with some facing each other and designed for comfortable seating. There could be strategically placed accessible toilets and more changing facilities. Spatial decisions could adopt carbon-neutral thinking, awareness of sea-level rising and climate disruption. For instance, electricity generating pathways, more water fountains, and re-use of local materials could be incentivised. Foremost, cities could have women increasingly represented through street names and art forms.

There is no single image of the ideal city designed by women, rather it is a mosaic of visions that could be leveraged by women themselves, co-evolved by residents, urban planners, policy makers, developers, retailers and communities. Since fostering gender equality is a fundamental trend of the 21st century and an essential aspect of good urbanism, this is an open invitation for our generation of women, and those of the future, to embrace the exciting, liberating and unprecedented prospects that come from designing cities that work for all.

9 | Afterword: Storylines

'Every word a woman writes changes the story of the world,
revises the official version.'
~ Carolyn See ~

Perth Storyline

Perth is a city in central Scotland, resting on the banks of the
River Tay – the largest river in the UK in terms of water
volume. The Tay has always been a significant actor in Perth's
rich storyline, with archaeological evidence suggesting that
people lived next to river crossings since the Mesolithic era,
8.000 years ago. The city's public parks of North Inch and
South Inch were created along the river, by reclaiming land
from swamp.

Perth is a walled medieval town characterised by a relatively
compact city centre with a variety of townscape characteristics,
including areas of Georgian and Victorian construction.[272] While
maintaining a significant degree of its historic built
environment, Perth serves as a commercial and cultural centre
for inhabitants of neighbouring towns and rural areas.

The city's history is steeped in the politics and treacheries of the
nobility, with many significant battles between Highland clans
and over Scottish independence fought in its territory. It was
tradition for Scotland's monarchs to be crowned in Perth,

where the Stone of Scone (also known as the Stone of Destiny) acted as an ancient symbol of royalty that witnessed the inauguration of many Scottish kings. The stone was seized by King Edward I of England in 1296 and only officially returned to Scotland in 1996. Even to this day, it is tradition for monarchs to be crowned in its presence, as enacted during King Charles III's recent coronation.

Known, unknown and fictitious women have enriched chapters of Perth's history. One of the best known is Catherine Glover, heroine of the novel *The Fair Maid of Perth*, written by Sir Walter Scott in 1828.[273] Today she is recognised by a bronze statue on the High Street where she sits on a bench with a book in her lap.

Perth was the stage for an important suffragette protest in the early 1900s, which was held to denounce Perth's prison treatment of suffragette prisoners, who were force-fed to nullify their hunger striking strategy. Later, in a supposedly unrelated event in 1914, Suffragettes targeted the Stone of Destiny and the coronation chair to agitate in favour of women's rights at Westminster Abbey.[274] Using militant tactics, they exploded a bomb that damaged the top of the chair and detached small particles of the stonework.[275]

During World War I, women from Perth played a significant role in the war effort. While many nurses cared for injured soldiers at Perth War Hospital, Jean Valentine became a dedicated Bombe operator. The Bombe played a pivotal role in decrypting the Enigma code used by German forces, revealing daily encryption details, allowing messages to be intercepted and decoded. Jean Valentine, along with many of her co-workers, kept her war effort secret until the mid-1970s.[276]

Perth is preparing for the return of the Stone of Destiny. One of the most iconic historical objects in Scotland, the news of its return has been widely welcomed as it is expected to attract numerous visitors to the area, creating significant uplift for tourism. The her/his story of Perth served as a backdrop for the walking interviews I conducted with women who lived and viewed Perth through contemporary eyes.

Portobello Storyline

Portobello lies on the east coast of Scotland, about four miles east of Edinburgh city centre. The neighbourhood possesses a seaside identity with a distinct town centre, a residential area, a long sea-front promenade, and a reclaimed and improved beach.

Portobello's name derives from the historic port of Puerto Bello in Panama, named 'Beautiful Port' by Christopher Columbus in 1502.[277] The Panamanian port was a centre for the silver trade and was attacked by the British navy on a number of occasions. In 1739, the British captured the city in a famous battle. George Hamilton, a sailor involved in the battle, later built a cottage near Edinburgh called 'Portobello Hut'. This hut became a stopover for travellers between Edinburgh and London, and by the 1750s, a small settlement called Portobello emerged around it.[278]

Portobello has been designated an outstanding conservation area due to its rich and varied Georgian, Victorian and Edwardian architecture.[279] While the vehicle-free Promenade reinforces the coastal resort character with cafés and amusement arcades, the High Street provides the area's commercial focus. The remainder constitutes Portobello's residential zone, including the fine Georgian and Victorian villas and tenements which contribute to the leafy suburban character.

Many remarkable women have lived in Portobello over the years, some widely known and others less so. Lucy Bethia

Walford, born in 1845, was a prolific writer and artist, known for her novels and artwork exhibited at the Royal Scottish Academy.[280] Helen Hopekirk, born in 1856, was a notable concert pianist and composer, blending Scottish folk music into her compositions.[281] While Marion Grieve, a prominent Scottish suffragette, gained renown for her support of various Portobello charities during the war.[282] She was remembered for collecting beach stones in Joppa and carrying them to demonstrations in her handbag.

Portobello was designated as a burgh by an Act of Parliament in 1833 and sixty years later became part of Edinburgh. The population rose sharply over the decades, through various waves of economic activities such as the establishment of brick, glass and pottery works, and the discovery of mineral wells.[283] The borough was at its peak as a sea-side resort in the late 19th century and today is experiencing a resurgence – as narrated by women to me during walking interviews.

Wester Hailes Storyline

Wester Hailes is a housing estate located 4 miles southwest of Edinburgh's city centre. Built on 297 acres of former agricultural land, the area was substantially developed in the late 1960s, a time when modernist planning, high-rise and high-density tower blocks were at their zenith.

In the rush to develop functional design solutions, compromises were made in both the design and construction materials of the dwellings – which cannot even with hindsight be forgiven.[284] The challenging living conditions of the original development ignited a rebellious community spirit, with residents having to contend with issues such indoor dampness, poor sound insulation, balcony leaks, and occasional flooding. The public realm was no less challenging, characterised by poorly lit streets and walkways, and windy, pointless, lonely, and dangerous open spaces empty of convivial locations for the community to gather.

During this period, residents, in particular women, campaigned for more facilities where people could meet, groups could be run, and services delivered. Women proudly referred to their story of social activism; for instance, when creating 'The Harbour' in the 1970s, a place for women to take refuge, share skills and spend time together. As with other developments in Wester Hailes, when official channels paid no heed, the community designed their own solutions and oversaw the construction of seven huts, which are fondly remembered by those long-term residents I interviewed.

Wester Hailes is notable for possessing significant areas of green space, including Hailes Quarry Park and Westburn Woods. Most of the woodland is situated along the bypass or further away at the golf course. Although important for biodiversity and carbon sequestration, these areas are not accessible to local residents or only accessible for paying members of the golf course.[285] Likewise, the Union Canal passes alongside the settlement, but has no easy access.

Wester Hailes is currently facing the challenge of how to integrate various short and long-term regenerative efforts led by different actors and collectives at community, city and national levels. Within the area's continuous flow of decline and revitalisation, my study invited women representing generations of social change agents, to consider the extent to which these initiatives are truly rooted in the practical realities of their everyday lives.

Drumchapel Storyline

Drumchapel is a modernist social housing scheme in the north-west of Glasgow, constructed on greenfield land as part of

Glasgow's post-war overspill policy.[286] A significant amount of the area's housing remains higher density post-war stock; however, there has been a major programme of housing regeneration and demolitions, resulting in a mix of new flats, houses and large areas of vacant or derelict land.

Intended to house 34,000 people, it followed the modernist architectural trends of the time, with planners envisaging a self-contained township with its own town centre, shops, schools, churches, open spaces, and communal services to serve residents. However, none of this occurred within the timeline anticipated.[287] Indeed, with restricted travel options and a lack of amenities, shops or public houses, residents from the very beginning experienced physical isolation from central Glasgow, paving the way for a gradual process of 'internalisation of stigmatisation'.[288]

Between the 1950s and the 1970s, while men were working with the major multinational employers and the various shipyards on the Clyde, women managed their lives in what was once referred to as 'a desert with windows'.[289] A woman, describing living conditions in the 1989 film *Drumchapel the Frustration Game*, confided that 'nobody would stay here by choice'. When recession arrived in the 1970s and the multinationals left, a massive wave of unemployment deepened the social hardship in the area, which in turn had a destabilising impact on the community and local commerce. This was followed by recurrent interventionist policies and layers of regeneration activity.

Drumchapel possesses green spaces like the centrally-located Drumchapel Park, Garscadden Burn Park (Site of Importance for Nature Conservation), and Garscadden Wood with woodland trails and paths. Substantial areas of grassland can also be found in the south-west of the area; however, no amenities nor infrastructure exist. A community garden initiative, Growchapel, addresses mental health and anti-social behaviour concerns while promoting social connections through shared food cultivation.

The area has also been struggling with the impact of a mineshaft running directly beneath residential areas and roads, contributing to recurrent flooding affecting local homes and businesses.[290] Drumchapel is an oft-cited example in local and national discussions of a peripheral housing estate experiencing significant poverty and social problems, characterised by the degeneration of poorly constructed post-war housing. My study sought to hear the experiences of women on what makes Drumchapel unique.

Yorkhill & Kelvingrove Storyline

Yorkhill & Kelvingrove is an area located in the west end of Glasgow city centre, and home to voluntary groups of local people promoting the interests of the neighbourhood under the umbrella of Yorkhill & Kelvingrove Community Council. While Yorkhill is known for its famous hospitals and remains the location of the West Glasgow Ambulatory Care Hospital, Kelvingrove is renowned for Kelvingrove Park, home to the Kelvingrove Art Gallery and Museum.

Kelvingrove Park lies at the heart of the community and is a meeting point for residents and visitors, a route for pedestrians and cyclists to the city centre, and a favourite spot for students from Glasgow University. Acting as an important green space forming part of a corridor connected to other patches of green by way of the River Kelvin, the park provides an important habitat for wildlife, facilitating the passage of many species, such as kingfishers, grey squirrels, red foxes, and the brown rats.

In terms of the built environment, Kelvingrove is part of the Kelvingrove Park conservation area of special architectural or historic interest, with many of its townhouses and tenements dating from the mid- to late-19th century being listed buildings.[291] The area is also home to several religious and institutional organisations, such as Om Hindu Mandir and the Gurdwara Singh Sabba temples, the Baitur Rahman mosque, as well as the Tron Church at Kelvingrove and the Glasgow Gaelic School.

The area aspires to become a Cycling Village and Scotland's most accessible community, encouraging more people to walk, wheel and cycle for short everyday journeys.[292] Whilst providing healthier streets and places for everyone, the Cycling Village project aligns with the City Council's strategic plan to create an active travel network covering the entirety of the city.

In recent years, Yorkhill & Kelvingrove has undergone a process of gentrification, metamorphosing from a disadvantaged neighbourhood into 'an-up-and-coming area'. Following a notable increase in visitors, the upsurge in construction of student accommodation and a recent increase in the number of local businesses, Yorkhill & Kelvingrove is becoming one of the Glasgow's most desirables places to live. Furthermore, there is a burgeoning arts scene with numerous independent artists collaborating and enriching the community. Women reflected on the different scenarios connected to the ongoing discussions about redeveloping the hospital area. Some expressed a desire for co-housing initiatives to retain families in the area, reduce population turnover and foster a stronger sense of community.

Glossary of terms

Access-Regress-Transfer Scheme: A transportation strategy ensuring convenient access, smooth entry/exit, and seamless transfers between modes for an efficient and connected travel experience.

Active Travel: Travelling with a purpose using your own energy. Generally, this means walking, cycling, wheeling and utilising non-motorised scooters to travel for any purpose.

Anthropocentric: A concept that places humans at the centre or as the primary focus of consideration and value. It is a viewpoint that primarily considers human interests, needs, and welfare, often prioritising them over the well-being of other species or the environment.

Blue Space: Outdoor environments, either natural or built, that prominently feature water bodies. It includes bodies of water such as rivers, lakes, ponds, reservoirs, canals, waterfalls, and even coastal areas like beaches and shorelines.

Co-evolving mutualism: A symbiotic relationship where two or more species evolve together, benefiting each other in a mutually advantageous way.

Data Disaggregation: The process of separating or disaggregating data into distinct categories or components for analysis or presentation.

Green Space: Any area of vegetated land, urban or rural. These spaces are intentionally designed or naturally occurring and serve various purposes, including biodiversity support, recreational, ecological, and aesthetic. Green spaces can take on various forms, including parks, gardens, woods, nature reserves, playing fields, and community allotments.

Perceived Safety: Individual's subjective assessment or feeling of being safe or secure in a specific environment or situation. It is based on a person's feelings, beliefs, and judgments about the level of safety or danger they perceive, regardless of the actual level of risk.

Reflexivity: The process of reflecting on oneself, one's actions, and one's assumptions. It involves being aware of and critically examining one's own perspectives, biases, and influences in relation to a particular situation or context.

Regenerative Development: A process of harmonising human activities with the continuing evolution of life on our planet–a process that also develops our own potential as humans. As an approach in practice, it seeks to enable human communities to come back into life-giving alignment with the natural living systems that support them.

Tokenism: Policy or practice of making minimal or symbolic efforts to include members of underrepresented groups in order to create an appearance of diversity or inclusion without addressing deeper issues of inequality or discrimination.

UN Sustainable Development Goals: A set of global goals established by the United Nations to address social, economic, and environmental challenges including those related to poverty, inequality, climate change, environmental degradation, peace and justice and promote sustainable development worldwide.

Categorisation of 33 Leverage Points

	Leverage Points	Places to Intervene	Category
1	Cultivating biophilia	Mindset	Mental Models
2	Developing spaces for gathering and belonging	The power to add, change, evolve or self-organise system structure	System Structure
3	Designing urban extensions while evolving the whole	The power to add, change, evolve or self-organise system structure	System Structure
4	Shifting from a mentality of maintenance to an attitude of care	Goals of the system	System Structure
5	Redistributing land use and budget allocation for equality and gendered landscapes	Rules of the system via parameters	System Structure Parameters
6	Creating conditions for wildness	The power to add, change, evolve or self-organise system structure	Parameters System Structure
7	Devising a library of women-tailored bike saddles	The structure of information flows	System Structure
8	Growing and foraging for health and wellbeing	The power to add, change, evolve or self-organise system structure	System Structure

9	Designing adventurous playgrounds for children and carers	The power to add, change, evolve or self-organise system structure	System Structure
10	Working with men to redistribute power, balance representation and transform legal and planning systems	Goals of the system	Mental Models
11	Building confidence through easy-to-access self-defence training, and seminars on rights of women and domestic violence	The structure of information flows	System Structure
12	Improving natural surveillance by design	Self-reinforcing positive feedback loops	Feedback Loops
13	Scheduling regular patrol walks by 'wardens who belong'	Self-reinforcing positive feedback loops	Feedback Loops
14	Making practical cycle awareness training mandatory for drivers	Rules of the system	System Structure
15	Encouraging active travel as a way of life	Mindset	Mental Models
16	Rethinking the bus fare system for trip chaining and redesigning bus for encumbered travel	The power to add, change, evolve or self-organise system structure	Parameters System Structure
17	Designing fresh air routes and low emissions zones from women's and infants' perspectives	The power to add, change, evolve or self-organise system structure	System Structure

18	Promoting early interventions and co-creating values-based educational pathways	The structure of Information flows	System Structure
19	Expanding the use of public space in the evenings by creating favourable bio-cultural-spatial conditions	Goals of the system	Mental Models
20	Co-developing sympathetic infrastructure enabling sense of co-ownership and care	The power to add, change, evolve or self-organise system structure	System Structure
21	Maximising use of available local resources available in urban interventions	The structure of material stocks and flows	Parameters
22	Practising a culture of deep listening in the design and development of local plans	Self-reinforcing positive feedback loops	Feedback Loops
23	Fostering regenerative tourism that enhances the bio-cultural-spatial uniqueness of place	The structure of information flows	System Structure
24	Adopting 20-minute neighbourhoods	Mindset	Mental Models
25	Co-creating transitional safeguarding public spaces for young women	Rules of the system	System Structure
26	Combining gender and nature-based approaches to transform urban environments	Goal of the system	Mental Models
27	Infusing beauty in cities' form and function	Goal of the system	Mental Models

28	Reconnecting broken links	The power to add, change, evolve or self-organise system structure	System Structure
29	Promoting the use of electric bikes	Rules of the system	System Structure
30	Refurbishing pavements to accommodate high heels	Rules of the system	System Structure
31	Delineating and flowing through cycling infrastructure	The structure of material stocks and flows	Parameters
32	Purpose-building inter-generational housing	Rules of the system The structure of material stocks and flows	System Structure Parameters
33	Co-designing places with (not only for) teenage girls	The structure of information flows	System Structure

Bibliography

Chapter One

[1] Greed, C. (1994), *Women and Planning: Creating Gendered Realities*. Routledge.

[2] Sassem, S. (2016). Built Gendering. Harvard Design Magazine. N.41, Family Planning.

[3] Beebeejaun, Y. (2017). Gender, urban space, and the right to everyday life. *Journal of Urban Affairs*, 39:3, pp. 323-334.

[4] East, M. (2019), Mapping the 'Presency' of Women in Cities. *Ecocycles Journal*, 5:2. pp. 1-5.

[5] UN Women (2019). *Progress on the Sustainable Development Goals: The gender snapshot 2019*. UN Department of Economic and Social Affairs. Statistics Division.

[6] UN-Habitat (2014). *Gender Equality Action Plan (2014-2019)*. UN-Habitat. 019/15E.

[7] World Bank (2020). *World Bank Handbook for Gender-Inclusive Urban Planning and Design*. International Bank for Reconstruction and Development. The World Bank.

[8] OECD (2021) *Gender and the Environment: Building Evidence and Policies to Achieve the SDGs*. OECD Publishing, Paris.

[9] URBACT EU (2022). Gender Equal Cities Report. [online] Available at: https://urbact.eu/gender-equal-cities-2022

[10] World Bank (2020).

[11] Damyanovic, D. & Zibell, B. (2013). Is there still gender on the agenda for spatial planning theories? Attempt to an integrative approach to generate gender-sensitive planning theories. *The Planning Review*, 49:4, pp. 25-36.

[12] CIESIN, IFPRI, CIAT (2011) Global Rural-Urban Mapping Project, Version 1 (GRUMPv1): Urban Extents Grid. NASA Socioeconomic Data and Applications Center (SEDAC).

[13] UN-Habitat (2021). Climate Change [online] Available at: https://unhabitat.org/topic/climate-change

[14] World Resources Institute, C40 & ICLEI (2021). GHG Protocol standard for cities. *An Accounting and Reporting Standard for Cities,* Version 1.1.

[15] Girardet, H. (2008). *Cities People Planet: Urban Development and Climate Change*. Wiley.

[16] United Nations Department of Economic and Social Affairs (2018). *Revision of World Urbanization Prospects: The 2018 Revision.* UNDESA. [online] Available at: https://population.un.org/wup/

[17] Sanford, C. (2016). What is Regeneration? Part 2. Living Structured Wholes. [online] Available at: https://carolsanfordinstitute.com/what-is-regeneration-part-

[18] du Plessis, C. (2012). Towards a regenerative paradigm for the built environment. *Building Research & Information*, 40:1, pp. 7-22.

[19] Robinson, J. & Cole, R.J. (2015). Theoretical underpinnings of regenerative sustainability. *Building Research & Information*, 43:2, pp. 133-143.

[20] Margolin, V. & Margolin, S. (2002). A "Social Model" of Design: Issues of Practice and Research. *Design Issues, MIT Press,* 18: 4. pp 24-30.

[21] Mang, P. & Haggard, B. (2016). *Regenerative Development & Design: A Framework for Evolving Sustainability.* Wiley.

[22] Mang, P. & Reed, B. (2012). Designing from place: A regenerative framework and methodology. *Building Research & Information*, 40: 1, pp. 23-38.

[23] Jacobs, J. (2016). *Jane Jacobs: The Last Interview and Other Conversations.* Melville House Publishing.

[24] de Beauvoir, S. (1949). *The Second Sex.* 2nd Edition. New York: The Modern Library.

[25] Listerborn, C. (2007). Who speaks? And who listens? The relationship between planners and women's participation in local planning in a multi-cultural urban environment. *GeoJournal,* 70:1, pp. 61-74.

Chapter Two

[26] Spain, D. (1992). *Gendered Spaces.* University of North Carolina Press.

[27] Kern, L. (2020). *Feminist City.* Verso.

[28] Bondi, L. & Rose, D. (2003). Constructing gender, constructing the urban: A review of Anglo-American feminist urban geography. *Gender, Place and Culture: A Journal of Feminist Geography*, 10:3, pp. 229-245.

[29] Collinge, C. (2005). The difference between society and space: nested scales and the returns of spatial fetishism. *Environment and Planning D: Society and Space*, Vol. 23, pp. 189-206.

[30] Keigher, S. M. (1993). Review of Discrimination by Design: A Feminist Critique of the Man-Made Environment.; The Sphinx in the City: Urban Life, the Control of Disorder, and Women, by Weisman L.K & Wilson E. *Contemporary Sociology*, 22: 2, pp. 173- 175.

[31] Hayden, D. (1981). The Grand Domestic Revolution. The MIT Press.

[32] Hayden, D. (1981)

[33] Agrest, D., Conway, P., & Weisman, L.K. (1996). *The Sex of Architecture.* Abrams.

[34] Torre, S. (2002). Claiming the Public Space, The Mothers of Plaza de Mayo. *Gender Space Architecture- An Interdisciplinary Introduction*, Chapter 19, pp. 140-145.

[35] Convention on the Elimination of all Forms of Discrimination against Women (1979). [online]. Available at: https://www.ohchr.org/EN/ProfessionalInterest/Pages/CEDAW.aspx

[36] Wilson, E. (1991). *The Sphinx in the City: Urban Life, the Control of Disorder, and Women*. Virago.

[37] Bondi, L. & Rose, D. (2003).

[38] Collinge, C. (2005).

[39] Wilson, E. (1991).

[40] van den Berg, M. (2012). City Children and Genderfied Neighbourhoods: The New Generation as Urban Regeneration Strategy. *International Journal of Urban and Regional Research*, 37: 2, pp. 367-823.

[41] Fincher, R. and Jacobs, J. M. (1998). *Cities of Difference*. The Guilford Press.

[42] Wilson, E. (1991).

[43] Jacobs, J. (1961) *The Death and Life of Great American Cities*. Vintage Books. pp. 432.

[44] Derrida, J. (1978). *Writing and Difference*. Chicago: The University of Chicago Press.

[45] Maturana, H. R. (1990). Biology of Language: The Epistemology of Reality. In: G.A. Miller & E. Lenneberg (eds.) *Psychology and Biology of Language and Thought: Essays in Honor of Eric Lenneberg*. New York: Academic Press. pp. 27-63.

[46] Freire, P. (1970). *Pedagogy of the Oppressed*. Continuum International Publishing Group.

[47] Oxford Dictionary (2019). Symbiosis [online] Available at: https://www.oxfordlearnersdictionaries.com/definition/english/symbiosis

Chapter Three

[48] Regenesis Group (2017). The Regenerative Practitioner. Systemic Frameworks. Regenesis Group, Inc.

[49] Einstein, A. (1935). *The Word as I See It*. Philosophical Library.

[50] Christy. L.F. (2007). Awakening from Newton's Sleep and the Sleep of Cybernetics. *Academia.Edu*. The George Washington University.

[51] Blake, W. (1802). *Letter to Thomas Butt*. Ed. by Geoffrey Keynes, The Macmillan Company. Copyright 1956.

[52] Kuhn, T. (1962). *The Structure of Scientific Revolutions*. University of Chicago Press.

[53] Amissah, M., Gannon, T. & Monat, J. (2020). What is Systems Thinking? Expert Perspectives from the WPI Systems Thinking Colloquium. *Systems,* 8:1, p. 6.
[54] Cabrera, D., Midgley, G. & Cabrera, L. (2021). *The Four Waves of Systems Thinking. Handbook of Systems Thinking.* Routledge.
[55] Meadows, D. (2008). *Thinking in Systems.* Chelsea Green Publishing.
[56] Bateson, N. (2022). What is Warm Data? [online]. Available at: https://batesoninstitute.org/warm-data/
[57] Campbell, K. (2018). *Making Massive Small Change.* Chelsea Green Publishing.

Chapter Four

[58] Meadows, D. (1999). Leverage Points- Places to Intervene in Systems. *Academy for Systems Change.* The Donella Meadows Project.
[59] Meadows, D. (1999).
[60] Archimedes. The Library of History of Diodorus Siculus, Fragments of Book XXVI, as translated by F. R. Walton. Loeb Classical Library (1957) Vol. XI.
[61] Fuller, B. (1982). *Critical Path.* St. Martin's Publishing Group.
[62] Meadows, D. (1999). P. 169
[63] Meadows, D. (1999). P. 169

Chapter Five

[64] Meadows, D. (1999). P. 169
[65] Gold, J. R. (1998). Creating the Charter of Athens: CIAM and the Functional City, 1933-43. *The Town Planning Review,* 69:3, pp. 225-247.
[66] Sánchez de Madariaga, I. & Roberts. M. (2013). *Fair Shared Cities: The Impact of Gender Planning in Europe.* Ashgate.
[67] Bosman, J. (1993). *Funktionale Stadt?* Werk, Bauen und Wohnen, Vol. 4, pp. 6-7.
[68] Curtis, W. (1986). *Le Corbusier: Ideas and Forms.* Oxford, Phaidon.
[69] Harvey, D. (1989). *The Condition of Postmodernity: An Enquiry into the Origins of Cultural Change.* Oxford, Blackwell.
[70] Greed, C. (1994).
[71] Fainstein, S.S. & Servon, L.J. (eds.) (2007). Gender and Planning: A Reader. *Urban Geography,* 28:3, pp. 1-14.
[72] van den Berg, M. (2018). The discursive uses of Jane Jacobs for the genderfying city: Understanding the productions of space for post-Fordist gender notions. *Urban Studies,* 55:4, pp. 751-766.
[73] Ungard-Benne, B. C. & Mang, P. (2015). Working Regeneratively Across Scales— Insights from Nature Applied to the Built Environment. *Journal of Cleaner Production,* Vol. 109, pp. 42-52.
[74] Mang, P. & Haggard, B. (2016).
[75] Wahl, D.C. (2016). *Designing Regenerative Cultures.* Triarchy Press.

[76] Regenesis Group (2017).
[77] Girardet, H., Schurig, S, Leidreiter, A. & Woo, F. (2013). Towards the Regenerative City. *The World Future Council*. Climate and Energy Commission Council.
[78] Woo, F. (2013). Regenerative urban development as a prerequisite for the future of cities. The Guardian. [online] https://www.theguardian.com/sustainable-business/regenerative-urban-development-future-cities
[79] Reed, B. (2007). Shifting from 'sustainability' to regeneration. *Building Research & Information*, 35:6. pp. 674-680.
[80] Regenesis Group (2017).
[81] Regenesis Group (2017).
[82] Scientific American (2012). Snappy Science: Stretched Rubber Bands Are Loaded with Potential Energy! [online] Available at: https://www.scientificamerican.com/article/bring-science-home-rubber-bands-energy
[83] Regenesis Group (2017).
[84] Regenesis Group (2017).
[85] Regenesis Group (2017).

Chapter Six
[86] Anderson, J.M., Adey, P. & Bevan, P. (2010). Positioning place: Polylogic approaches to research methodology. *Qualitative Research*, 10:5, pp. 589-604.
[87] Spence, C. (2020). Senses of place: architectural design for the multisensory mind. *Cognitive Research*, Vol. 5, p. 46.
[88] Clark, A. & Emmel, N. (2010). Using walking interviews. *National Centre for Research Methods*. University of Manchester.
[89] METRAC (2022). Working to end gender-based violence across communities. [online] Available at: https://metrac.org
[90] Whitzman, C., Shaw, M., & Andrew, C. (2009). The effectiveness of women's safety audits. *Security Journal*, Vol. 22, pp. 205-218.
[91] Owen, H. (1977). *Open Space Technology: A User's Guide*. Berrett-Koehler Publishers.

Chapter Seven
[92] Low, S.M. & Altman, I. (1992). *Place Attachment*. New York: Plenum Press.
[93] Stedman, R.C. (2002). Toward a Social Psychology of Place: Predicting Behavior from Place-Based Cognitions, Attitude, and Identity. *Environment and Behavior*, 34:5, pp. 561–581.
[94] Cambridge Dictionary (2022). Biophilia [online] Available at: https://dictionary.cambridge.org dictionary/ english/biophilia

[95] Alemán, G. (2000). *El Parque Municipal Garcia Sanabria.* Exmo Ayuntamiento de Santa Cruz de Tenerife.

[96] Sanford, C. (2022). *Indirect Work.* InterOctave.

[97] Oliver, M. (1986). *Dream Work.* The Atlantic Monthly Press.

[98] Montessori, M. (1909). *The Montessori Method.* Cosimo Classics.

[99] Piaget, J. (1952). *The Origins of Intelligence in Children.* International Universities Press.

[100] Proshansky, H.M. (1978). The City and Self-Identity. *Environment and Behavior,* 10:2, pp. 147–169.

[101] Ryden, K.C. (1993). *Mapping the Invisible Landscape: Folklore, Writing, and the Sense of Place.* University of Iowa Press.

[102] Low, S.M. & Altman, I. (1992).

[103] Pretty, G.H., Chipuer, H.M., & Bramston, P. (2003). Sense of place amongst adolescents and adults in two rural Australian towns: The discriminating features of place attachment, sense of community and place dependence in relation to place identity. *Journal of Environmental Psychology, 23:3.*

[104] Neal, P. (ed) (2003). *Urban villages and the making of communities.* Taylor & Francis.

[105] Hunt, E. (2019). City with a female face: how modern Vienna was shaped by women. The Guardian. [online] Available at: https://www.theguardian.com/cities/2019/may/14/city-with-a-female-face-how-modern- vienna-was-shaped-by-women

[106] Clarke, K. (2018). The Sexist Streets of the World. [online] Available at: https://googlemapsmania.blogspot.com/2018/05/the-sexist-streets-of-world.html

[107] NHS (2015). *The Royal Hospital for Sick Children Celebrating a proud history 1882-2015.* NHS Greater Glasgow & Clyde.

[108] Robertson, E, (1972). *The Yorkhill Story: The History of The Royal Hospital for Sick Children, Glasgow.* Yorkhill and Associated Hospitals Board of Management.

[109] Tronto, J.C., & Fisher, B. (1990) Toward a Feminist Theory of Caring. In E. Abel & M Nelson (eds). *Circles of Care.* Albany, NY: SUNY Press. pp. 36-54.

[110] Lucas, K., Walker, G., Eames, M., Fay, H., & Poustie, M. (2004). Environment and social justice: rapid research and evidence review. *London, UK Policy Studies Institute.*

[111] Col.lectiu Punt 6 (2020). [online] Available at https://www.punt6.org/es/es-punt-6/

[112] Valdivia, B. (2017). Towards a paradigm shift: the caring city. *Barcelona Metròpolis.* Edition núm. 104.

[113] Wheatley, M. J. (2002). *Turning to One Another: Simple Conversations to Restore Hope to the Future.* San Francisco: Berrett-Koshler Publishers, Inc.

[114] Shiva, V, (2005). Earth Democracy: Justice, Sustainability and Peace. London: Zed Books.

[115] URBACT (2020). Umeå [online] Available at: https://urbact.eu/umea

[116] Gustafsson. L. (2017). Umeå – Gender equality at the heart of the city. URBACT EU. [online] Available at: https://www.blog.urbact.eu/2017/12/umea-gender-equality-at-the- heart-of-the-city/

[117] Meadows, D. (1999).

[118] Damyanovic, D., Reinwald, F., & Weikmann, A. (2013). *Manual for Gender Mainstreaming in Urban Planning and Urban Development.* Urban Development and Planning. The City of Vienna.

[119] Dimitrova, A. (2021). Lyon to adopt the first "gender budget" in France. The Mayor EU. [online] Available at: https://www.themayor.eu/en/a/view/lyon-to-adopt-the-first-gender-budget-in-france- 7393

[120] Regional Government of Andalusia (2010). *G+ Project A methodology for using public budgeting to improve gender equality.* Ministry of Finance and Public Administration.

[121] Obama, B. (2016). The Budget Message of the President. Office of the Press Secretary. The White House.

[122] De Sousa Santos, B (1998). Participatory Budgeting in Porto Alegre: Toward a Redistributive Democracy. *Politics & Society,* 26:4, pp. 461-510.

[123] Schulte to Bühne, H., Pettorelli, N., & Hoffmann, M. (2022). The policy consequences of defining rewilding. *Ambio,* Vol. 51, pp 93–102.

[124] WWF (2022). What is the sixth mass extinction and what can we do about it? [online] Available at: https://www.worldwildlife.org/stories/what-is-the-sixth-mass-extinction-and-what-can-we-do-about-it

[125] Kopenawa, D. & Senra, E.B. (2023). Precisamos falar sobre a beleza dos Yanomamis. Instituto Socio-Ambiental [online] Available at: https://www.socioambiental.org/noticias-socioambientais/precisamos-falar-sobre-beleza-dos-yanomami

[126] Parc de La Citadel (2023) Lille's Citadel, a complete history.[online] Available at https://parcdelacitadelle.lille.fr/en/node/930/heritage

[127] Le Parisien (2023). Près de Valenciennes, les autorités à la recherche d'un 'grand félin' aperçu plusieurs fois [online] Available at https://www.leparisien.fr/faits-divers/pres-de-valenciennes-les-autorites-a-la-recherche-dun-grand-felin-apercu-plusieurs-fois

[128] Paciaroni, S. (2022) How Yorkhill Green Spaces are repopulating Glasgow's West End with insects. Glasgow Times. [Online]. Available at: https://www.glasgowtimes.co.uk/news/scottish-news/20135518.yorkhill-green-spaces-repopulating-glasgows-west-end-insects/

[129] Melbourne Department of Environment, Land, Water and Planning (2015). *Plan Melbourne Refresh 2017-2050*. Victoria State Government.

[130] Heinen, E., van Wee, B. & Maat, K. (2010). Commuting by bicycle: An overview of the literature. *Transport Reviews*, 30:1, pp 59–96.

[131] SUSTRANS (2022). Is separate equal? Single-sex cycling spaces and gender equality [online] Available at: https://www.sustrans.org.uk/our-blog/opinion/2022/august/is-separate-equal-single-sex-cycling-spaces-and-gender

[132] Leva, M.C., Ababio-Donkor, A., & Thimnu, A. (2021) Gender and Equality in Transport. *Proceedings of the 2021 Travel Demand Management Symposium*. Technological University Dublin.

[133] Heesch, K.C., Sahlqvist, S. & Garrard, J. (2012). Gender differences in recreational and transport cycling: a cross-sectional mixed-methods comparison of cycling patterns, motivators, and constraints. *Int J Behav Nutr Phys Act,* 9: 106.

[134] Broadbent, B. (2020) Finding a comfortable saddle. BBC Women's Hour. [online] Available at: https://www.bbc.co.uk/sounds/play/m000l8lh

[135] Women who Cycle (2019). Commonly asked question – What is the best women's bike saddle? [online] Available at: https://womenwhocycle.com/what-is-the-best-womens-bike-saddle/

[136] Perez, C.C. (2019). *Invisible Women - Exposing Data Bias in a Word Designed for Men*. Penguin Random House.

[137] Hollmann, V., Donath, T.W., Grammel, F., Himmighofen, T., Zerahn, U., & Leyer, I. (2020). From nutrients to competition processes: Habitat specific threats to Arnica montana L. populations in Hesse, Germany. *PLoS ONE*, 15:5.

[138] FAO (2021). Tracking progress on food and agriculture-related SDG indicators 2021: A report on the indicators under FAO custodianship. FAO. Rome.

[139] Davi Kopenawa Yanomami. Survival International. [online]. Available at: https://www.survivalinternational.org/articles/3512-DaviYanomami

[140] The National Society of Allotment and Leisure Gardens (2021). Brief History of Allotments. [online] Available at: https://www.nsalg.org.uk/allotment-info/brief-history-of-allotments/

[141] The National Society of Allotment and Leisure Gardens (2021).

[142] Edible Estates. Clovenstone Neighbourhood Garden. [online]. Available at: https://www.edibleestates.co.uk/project/clovenstone-neighbourhood-garden/

[143] Lowry, C.A., Hollis, J. H., de Vries, A., Pan, B., Brunet, L. R., Hunt, J. R., Paton, J. F., van Kampen, E., Knight, D. M., Evans, A. K., Rook, G. A., & Lightman, S. L. (2007). Identification of an immune-responsive mesolimbocortical serotonergic system: Potential role in regulation of emotional behavior. *Neuroscience,* 146:2, pp. 756–772.

[144] Paddock, C (2007). *Soil Bacteria Work in Similar Way to Antidepressants*. Medical News Today.

[145] Barton, J., & Rogerson, M. (2017). The importance of greenspace for mental health. *BJPsych international*, 14:4, pp. 79–81.

[146] Grass Roots Remedies Cooperative (2023). [online] Available at: https://grassrootsremedies.co.uk

[147] Thomas, A. (2017). These New York Gardeners are Fighting the System by Growing Food. [online] Available at: https://www.thefader.com/2017/04/17/bronx-gardeners-empower-communities

[148] Gore, S. (2020). Meet the BIPOC Farmers Cultivating Green Spaces in NYC. [online] Available at: https://www.teenvogue.com/story/meet-the-bipoc-farmers-cultivating-green-spaces-in-nyc

[149] Farm School NY (2023). Training urban agriculture activists and advocates [online] Available at https://www.farmschoolnyc.org

[150] UNICEF (1989). UN Convention on the Rights of the Child. Adopted by the General Assembly on of 20 November 1989. (Resolution 44/25).

[151] van Vleet, M., Helgeson V.S., & Berg, C. A. (2019). The importance of having fun: Daily play among adults with type 1 diabetes. *J Soc Pers Relat*, 1:36, pp. 3695-3710.

[152] Sinclair, M. (2016). *Well Played – The Ultimate Guide to Awakening Your Family's Playful Spirit*. HarperCollins Publishers.

[153] Holmes, R. & Hart, T. (2022). Exploring the Connection between Adult Playfulness and Emotional Intelligence. *The Journal of Play in Adulthood*, 4:1, pp. 28-51.

[154] Wester Hailes Sentinel (2023) From there… to here. The Venchie Story [online] Available at: https://www.bbc.co.uk/sounds/play/m000l8lh

[155] Kambas, A., Antoniou, P., Xanthi, G., Heikenfeld, R., Taxildaris, K., & Godolias, G. (2004). Accident prevention through development of coordination in kindergarten children. *Deutsche Zeitschrift für Sportmedizin*, 55:2, pp. 44-47.

[156] Brussoni, M., Olsen, L. L., Pike, I., & Sleet, D. A. (2012). Risky play and children's safety: balancing priorities for optimal child development. *International journal of environmental research and public health*, 9:9, pp. 3134–3148.

[157] Play England (2007). Charter for Play. [online] Available at: https://www.playengland.org.uk/charter-for-play

[158] The Crown Prosecution Service (2022). CPS sets out the law on street-based sexual harassment [online] Available at: https://www.cps.gov.uk/cps/news/cps-sets-out-law-street-based-sexual-harassment

[159] UK Public General Acts (1997). Protection from Harassment Act 1997. [online] Available at: https://www.legislation.gov.uk/ukpga/1997/40/contents

[160] de Beauvoir, S. (1949). *The Second Sex*. 2nd Edition. New York: The Modern Library.

[161] METRAC (2022).

[162] Thompson, M.E. (2014). Empowering Self-Defense Training. *Violence Against Women*, 20:3, pp. 351-359.

[163] Telsey, N. (1981). Karate and the feminist resistance movement. In: F. Delacoste & F. Newman (eds.) Fight back! Feminist resistance to male violence. Minneapolis, MN: Cleis Press. pp. 184-196.

[164] Hollander, J. A. (2016). The importance of self-defense training for sexual violence prevention. *Feminism & Psychology*, 26:2, pp. 207-226.

[165] Barbauld, A. L. (1773). The Rights of Woman. Poems.

[166] Jacobs, J. (1961).

[167] Lee, J.S., Park S., & Jung, S. (2016). Effect of Crime Prevention through Environmental Design (CPTED) Measures on Active Living and Fear of Crime. *Sustainability*, 8.872.

[168] Newman, O. (1972). *Defensible space: Crime Prevention through Urban Design*. Macmillan: New York, NY.

[169] Aatika, S. (2023) Why does a group of women walk at midnight in Delhi? TwoCirclesNet [online] Available at: https://twocircles.net/2023apr20/448795.html

[170] Diniz. M. (2019) O Policiamento Comunitário em Lisboa e a coprodução de segurança a nível local. *Conferência de Segurança Urbana*. Lisboa Polícia Municipal.

[171] Sustrans (2018). Are we nearly there yet? Exploring gender and active travel. Sustrans.

[172] Wendel-Vos, W., v,d. Berg, S., Giesbers, H., Harms. L., Kruize, H., & Staatsen, B. (2018). *Cycling in the Netherlands*. The National Institute for Public Health and Environment.

[173] Garrard, J., Handy, S. & Dill, J. (2012). Women and Cycling. In: J. Pucher & R. Buehler (eds.) *City Cycling*. Cambridge: MIT Press. pp. 211-234.

[174] Willeme, A. (2023). 7 things that will get you fined while cycling in the Netherlands. Dutch Review. [online] Available at: https://dutchreview.com/culture/things-that-will-get-you-fined-while-cycling-in-the-netherlands/

[175] Tennant, C. (2022). The world's cycling nation: How the Netherlands redesigned itself as a country fit for bikes. Euronews.

[176] InfraSisters (2023). [online] Available at: https://www.infrasisters.org.uk

[177] Bike for Good (2023) [online] Available at: https://www.bikeforgood.org.uk/get-cycling/cycle-training/

[178] Cycling Scotland (2022). Practical Cycle Awareness Training (PCAT) [online] Available at: https://www.cycling.scot/what-we-do/training/practical-cycle-awareness- training

[179] Government of Ireland (2020). What Active Travel Is. [online] Available at: https://www.gov.ie/en/campaigns/d96bd-active-travel/

[180] TCPA (2021). 20-Minute Neighbourhoods- Creating Healthier, Active, Prosperous Communities- An Introduction for Council Planners in England. *Town and Country Planning Association*.
[181] Hopkins, R. (2008). *The Transition Handbook: From Oil Dependency to Local Resilience*. UIT Cambridge Ltd.
[182] Sanderson, E.W. (2013). Time to escape the oil trap. *The Inquirer*. [online] Available at: https://www.inquirer.com/philly/opinion/inquirer/20130820_Time_to_escape_the_oil_t rap.html?outputType=amp
[183] Watts, M. (2021). There Will be Blood: Oil Curse, Fossil Dependency and Petro-Addiction. *New Formations*, Vol. 2021, No. 103, pp.10-42.
[184] Saeidizand, P., Fransen, K. & Boussauw, K. (2021). Revisiting car dependency: a worldwide analysis of car travel in global metropolitan areas. *Cities*, 120:6, 103467.
[185] Minster, C., Chlond, B., von Behren, S., & Hunecke, M. (2016). Mesurer les aspects subjectifs et objectifs de da dépendance automobile. *Swiss Mobility Conference*, Université de Lausanne.
[186] UK Department for Transport (2020). Trip Chaining: 2002-2014. National Travel Survey.
[187] Hine, J. & Mitchell, F. (2001) The Role of Transport in Social Exclusion in Urban Scotland. *Scottish Executive Research Unit*.
[188] Turner, T., Niemeier, D. (1997). Travel to work and household responsibility: new evidence. *Transportation*, Vol. 24, pp 397–419.
[189] Law, R. (1999). Beyond 'women and transport': towards new geographies of gender and daily mobility. *Prog. Hum. Geogr.*, Vol 23, pp. 567–588.
[190] Rosenbloom, S. (2006). Understanding women's and men's travel patterns. Research on Women's Issues in Transportation: Report of a Conference. *Transportation Research Board*, Washington, DC, pp. 7–28.
[191] Sandberg, L. & Röhnblom, M. (2016). Imagining the ideal city, planning the gender- equal city in Umeå, Sweden. *Gender, Place & Culture*, 23:12, pp. 1750-1762.
[192] Trivector Traffic (2020). *Equality and the transport system*. Vinnova Sweedish Innovation Agency.
[193] Equality and Human Rights Commission (2017). Wheelchair spaces on buses must be a priority, court rules. [online]. Available at: https://www.equalityhumanrights.com/en/our-work/news/wheelchair-spaces-buses-must-be-priority-court-rules
[194] Holman, C., Harrison, R., & Querol, X. (2015). Review of the efficacy of low emission zones to improve urban air quality in European cities. *Atmospheric Environment*, Vol. 111, pp 161-169.
[195] The High Line (2023). [online] Available at https://www.thehighline.org

[196] Sharma. A. & Kumar, P. (2022). Air pollution exposure assessment simulation of babies in a bike trailer and implication for mitigation measures. *Journal of Hazardous Materials Advances,* Vol. 5.

[197] Mums for Lungs (2023). [online] Available at: https://www.mumsforlungs.org

[198] Greater London Authority (2022). Mayor hails success of Schools Streets programme. [online] Available at: https://www.london.gov.uk/press-releases/mayoral/mayor-hails-success-of-schools-streets-programme

[199] Herefordshire Council (2023) Herefordshire Council considering introducing 'school streets' [online] Available at: https://yourherefordshire.co.uk/

[200] WHO (2021). *Global Air Quality Guidelines: particulate matter (PM2.5 and PM10), ozone, nitrogen dioxide, sulfur dioxide and carbon monoxide.* Centre for Environment & Health. World Health Organization.

[201] Leeds Festival of Kindness, Compassion and Wellbeing (2021). Kinder Leeds [online] Available at: https://kinderleeds.org

[202] da Silva, R. C. O. (2006). Reversing the Rite: Music, Dance, and Rites of Passage among Street Children and Youth in Recife, Brazil. *The World of Music- Music and Childhood: Creativity, Socialization, and Representation,* 48:1, pp. 83-97

[203] UNESCO (2020). *Artificial intelligence and gender equality: key findings of UNESCO's Global Dialogue.* UNESCO.

[204] Merriam-Webster Dictionary (2023). [online] Available at: https://www.merriam-webster.com/dictionary/passeggiata

[205] Listerborn, C. (2002). Understanding the geography of women's fear. In: L Bondi *et al., Subjectivities, Knowledges, and Feminist Geographies.* Rowman & Littlefield. pp. 34-43.

[206] Pain, R. H. (1997). Social Geographies of Women's Fear of Crime. *Transactions of the Institute of British Geographers,* 22:2, pp. 231–244.

[207] Etymology Dictionary (2022). Emancipate, [online] Available at: https://www.etymonline.com/word/emancipate

[208] Meadows, D. (1999).

[209] Berry, W. (1997). *The unsettling of America: Culture and agriculture.* Sierra Club Book.

[210] World Bank (2022). *Squaring the Circle: Policies from Europe's Circular Economy Transition.* World Bank.

[211] Circularity Gap Reporting Initiative (2023). The Circularity Gap Report. [online] Available at: https://www.circularity-gap.world/20232023

[212] Nicolli, V. (2015). Kelvingrove Park gates return. Glasgow Times. [online] Available at: https://www.glasgowtimes.co.uk/news/13303586.kelvingrove-park-gates-return/

213 Corbett, G. (2019). Bridge8 hub: canal social enterprise. Edinburgh and West Lothians Green [online] Available at: https://www.edinburghgreens.org.uk/blog/bridge8/

214 Newton, I. (1687). *Philosophiæ Naturalis Principia Mathematica.* Royal Society of London.

215 European Commission Directorate-General for Environment (2004). Reclaiming city streets for people. Chaos or quality of life? Publications Office.

216 Wheatley, M.J. (2002). *Turning to One Another: Simple Conversations to Restore Hope to the Future.* San Francisco: Berrett-Koshler Publishers, Inc.

217 Bellato, I., Frantzeskaki, N., & Nygaard, C. A. (2022). Regenerative tourism: a conceptual framework leveraging theory and practice. *Tourism Geographies,* 25:4, pp.1026-1046.

218 Pollock, A. (2023). Conscious Travel takes a new approach to tourism development in eight key ways. [online] Available at: http://www.conscious.travel/approach/

219 Pollock, A. (2023).

220 East, M. (2018). Current thinking on sustainable human habitat: the Findhorn Ecovillage case. *Ecocycles Journal,* 4:1, pp. 68–72.

221 Mairie de Paris (2022). Paris ville du quart d'heure, ou le pari de la proximité. Ville de Paris. [online] Available at: https://www.paris.fr/dossiers/paris-ville-du-quart-d-heure-ou-le-pari-de-la-proximite-37

222 Melbourne Department of Environment, Land, Water and Planning (2015).

223 City of Portland and Multnomah County (2015). *2015 Climate Action Plan.* Bureau of Planning and Sustainability, City of Portland. Office of Sustainability, Multnomah County.

224 Gunn, L.D., King T.L., Mavoa, S, Lamb K, Giles-Corti B., & Kavanagh A. (2017). Identifying destination distances that support walking trips in local neighbourhoods. *Journal of Transport and Health,* Vol. 5, pp. 133-141.

225 Christian, H.E., Fiona, C.B., Nicholas, J.M., Matthew, W.K., Mark, L.D., Paula, H., Anura, A., & Giles-Corti, B. (2011). How important is the land use mix measure in understanding walking behavior? Results from the RESIDE study. *Int. J. Behav. Nutr. Phys Act,* Vol. 8, p. 55.

226 Manaugh, K. & El-Geneidy, A.M. (2011). Validating Walkability Indices: How Do Different Households Respond to the Walkability of Their Neighbourhood? *Transportation Research Part D: Transport and Environment,* Vol. 16, pp. 309-315.

227 Thornton, L.E., Schroers, R.D., Lamb, K.E., Daniel, M., Ball, K., Chaix, B., Kestens, Y., Best, K., Oostenbach, L., & Coffee, N.T. (2022). Operationalising the 20-minute neighbourhood. *The international journal of behavioral nutrition and physical activity,* 19:1.

228 Melbourne Department of Environment, Land, Water and Planning (2015).

²²⁹ City of Portland and Multnomah County (2015).

²³⁰ Mairie de Paris (2022).

²³¹ Moreno, C., Allam, Z., Chabaud, D., Gall, C., & Pratlong, F. (2021). Introducing the '15-minute city': sustainability, resilience and place identity in future post-pandemic cities. *Smart Cities*, 4:1, pp. 93-111.

²³² RTPI Scotland (2021). Implementing 20 Minute Neighbourhoods in Planning Policy and Practice. [online] Available at: https://www.rtpi.org.uk/research/2021/march/20-minute-neighbourhoods/

²³³ Norberg-Hodge, H. (2019) *Local Is Our Future. Steps to an Economics of Happiness*. Local Futures

²³⁴ Make Cities Safer for Girls (2018). 8 Safety Demands from City Girls. Plan International UK. [online] Available at: https://plan-international.org/case-studies/8-safety-demands-from-city-girls/

²³⁵ d'Eaubonne, F. (1974) Feminism or Death. Verso Books

²³⁶ Wilson, E. (1991).

²³⁷ WWF (2023). Nature-Based Solutions. [online] Available at: https://wwf.panda.org/discover/our_focus/climate_and_energy_practice/what_we_do/nature_based_solutions_for_climate/

²³⁸ Francour, D. (2022), Nature-Based Solutions are False Climate Change Solutions: Indigenous Peoples Hold the True Solutions to Climate Change. Cultural Survival. [online] Available at: https://www.culturalsurvival.org/publications/cultural-survival-quarterly/nature-based-solutions-are-false-climate-change-solutions

²³⁹ Chan, F.K.S., Griffiths, J.A., Higgitt, D., Xu, S., Zhu,F., Tang, Y.T., Xu, Y. & Thorne, C.R. (2018) "Sponge City" in China—A breakthrough of planning and flood risk management in the urban context. *Land Use Policy*. Vol. 76, pp. 772-778.

²⁴⁰ Rosa, M. (2015) Movimento restaura postes para deixar bairros mais bonitos em Florianópolis. Ciclo Vivo. [online] Available at: https://ciclovivo.com.br/inovacao/inspiracao/movimento-restaura-postes-para-deixar-bairros-mais-bonitos-em-florianopolis/

²⁴¹ Mann, J. (2015). Towards a politics of whimsy: yarn bombing the city. *Area*, 47:1. pp. 65-72.

²⁴² Ayuntamiento de Alicante (2023). Basílica de Santa María [Online]. Available at: https://www.alicanteturismo.com/basilica-de-santa-maria/

²⁴³ Olabi, A.G., Wilberforce,T., Obaideen, K., Sayed,E.T., Shehata, N., Alami, A.H., & Abdelkareem,M.A.(2023) Micromobility: Progress, benefits, challenges, policy and regulations, energy sources and storage, and its role in achieving sustainable development goals. *International Journal of Thermofluids*, Vol. 17, No. 100292

[244] Berntsen, S., Malnes, L., Langåker, A., & Bere, E. (2017). Physical activity when riding an electric assisted bicycle. *The international journal of behavioral nutrition and physical activity*, Vol 14, Item 1, p.55.

[245] Vélib Metropol [online] Available at: https://www.velib-metropole.fr/en_GB/service

[246] Donkey Republic [online] Available at: https://www.donkey.bike/

[247] Encicla [online] Available at: https://encicla.metropol.gov.co

[248] Bae, Y.H., Ko, M., Park, Y.S., & Lee, S.M. (2015). Effect of revised high-heeled shoes on foot pressure and static balance during standing. *Journal of physical therapy science*, 27:4, pp. 1129–1131.

[249] Seoul Metropolitan Government (2014) *Women Friendly City Project.* Policies. Women & Family Policy Affairs.

[250] Maarou, M.A. (2015). The Impact of Wearing High Heels on Women's Health and Attractiveness: A Field Study. *Journal of Basic and Applied Scientific Research*, 5:8, pp. 54-61.

[251] Desai, S. (2022). Tracking the effects of high heels at work. Harvard Gazette [online] Available at: https://news.harvard.edu/gazette/story/2022/02/harvard-talk-examines-effects-of-high-heels-at-work/?utm_medium=Feed&utm_source=Syndication

[252] Goel, R., Oyebode, O., Foley L., Tatah, L, Millett, C., & Woodcock, J. (2022). Gender differences in active travel in major cities across the world *Transportation, Vol.* 50, pp. 733-749.

[253] Transport for London (2012). *Understanding the travel needs of London's diverse communities: Women.* Mayor of London.

[254] Sustrans (2018).

[255] Meadows, D. (1999).

[256] Sustrans (2018). Inclusive city cycling. Women: Reducing the Gender Gap. Bike Life. Sustrans.

[257] City of Copenhagen (2011). The City of Copenhagen's bicycle strategy, 2011–2025 [Online]. Available at: https://handshakecycling.eu/resources/citycopenhagen%E2%80%99s-bicyclestrategy-2011-2025

[258] Cycling Embassy of Denmark (2015). Bicycle statistics from Denmark, Report. *Cycling Embassy of Denmark*, Copenhagen.

[259] Christiania Bikes (2023) Our History. [Online]. Available at: https://www.christianiabikes.com/en/om-os/vores-historie/

[260] InfraSisters (2023).

[261] UNDESA (2023). UNDESA World Social Report 2023: Leaving No One Behind in An Ageing World. Department of Economic and Social Affairs. United Nations

²⁶² Das, M.B., Yuko, A., Chapman, T.B. & Jain, V. (2022). *Silver Hues: Building Age-Ready Cities*. World Bank, Washington, DC.
²⁶³ Japan Minister of Health, Labour and Welfare (2023). [Online]. Available at: https://www.mhlw.go.jp/english/database/
²⁶⁴ Centre for Public Impact (2018). Mehrgenerationenhäuser II in Germany. [Online]. Available at: https://www.centreforpublicimpact.org/case-study/mehrgenerationenhauser-germany
²⁶⁵ Teruel, An (2022). La caída de la natalidad en la provincia de Alicante acelera aún más el envejecimiento de la población. *Información*.
²⁶⁶ Garcia, S. & Marti, P. (2014). Intergenerational Architecture and Public Space. *ARQ*.
²⁶⁷ World Habitat Awards (2016) Municipal Project for Intergenerational Housing and Community Services in Alicante [online]. Available at: https://world-habitat.org/world-habitat-awards/winners-and-finalists/municipal-project-for-intergenerational-housing-and-community-services-in-alicante/
²⁶⁸ Walker, S. & Clark, I. (2023). Make Space for Girls 2023 Report. [Online]. Available at: https://www.makespaceforgirls.co.uk/resources/research-report-2023
²⁶⁹ Twenge, J.M. (2017) *iGen- Why Today's Super-Connected Kids Are Growing Up Less Rebellious, More Tolerant, Less Happy--and Completely Unprepared for Adulthood-and What That Means for the Rest of Us*. Atria Books.
²⁷⁰ Landscape Architecture Platform (2020) Bredäng Park – dance and play! [Online]. Available at: https://landezine.com/bredang-park-dance-and-play/

Chapter Eight
²⁷¹ Merriam-Webster Dictionary (2023) [online] Available at: https://www.merriam-webster.com/dictionary/elucidate

Chapter Nine
²⁷² Perth & Kinross Council (2008). Perth Central Conservation Area Appraisal. Perth & Kinross Council.
²⁷³ Scott, S.W. (1828). The Fair Maid of Perth. Caddel & Co.
²⁷⁴ HES (2016). 20 facts revealed about the Stone of Destiny. *Historic Environment Scotland*. [online] Available at: https://www.historicenvironment.scot/about-us/news/20-facts-revealed-about-the-stone-of-destiny/ [Accessed 20 March 2020].
²⁷⁵ The Morning Post (1914). Militant Anarchy – Bomb Explosion at the Abbey – Coronation Chair Damaged – No Arrests. The Life and Times of Florence Nightingale. Suffragette Newspaper Index.
²⁷⁶ National Museum of Computing (2019). Jean Valentine (1924-2019). [online] Available at: https://www.tnmoc.org/notes-from-the-museum/2019/6/18/jean-valentine- 1924-2019 [Accessed 15 February 2021].

277 Samos, A. (2014). Sandra Eleta in Portobelo. Guggenheim Museum. [online] Available at: https://www.guggenheim.org/blogs/map/sandra-eleta-in-portobelo[Accessed 22 May 2022].

278 Groome, F.H. (ed.) (1882-1885). The Ordnance Gazetteer of Scotland; a survey of Scottish topography, statistical, biographical, and historical, 2nd ed. London: William Mackenzie.

279 Edinburgh City Council (2000). Portobello Conservation Area Character Appraisal. Planning and Building Standards- Conservation Area Character Appraisals. The City of Edinburgh Council.

280 Scottish Women Writers (2020). Lucy Bethia Walford. [Online] Available at: https://www.scottishwomenwritersontheweb.net/writers-a-to-z/lucy-bethia-walford [Accessed 7 July 2021].

281 Steigerwalt, G. (2011). Helen Hopekirk, Scottish-American Pianist, Composer, and Pedagogue. The Leschetizky Association News Bulletin, 2010-11, pp 8-15.

282 Foley, A. & Munro, M. (2013). Portobello and the Great War. Amberley Publishing

283 Edinburgh City Council (2000). Portobello Conservation Area Character Appraisal. Planning and Building Standards- Conservation Area Character Appraisals. The City of Edinburgh Council.

284 Rowe, H. A. (2011). The Rise and Fall of Modernist Architecture. Inquiries Journal, Vol. 3, Issue 4.

285 Wester Hailes Community Trust (2022). Wester Hailes - A Local Place Plan. Urban Pioneers Ltd.

286 Paice, L. (2008). Overspill Policy and the Glasgow Slum Clearance Project in the Twentieth Century: From One Nightmare to Another? Reinvention: a Journal of Undergraduate Research, Vol. 1, Issue 1.

287 Craig, A. (2003). The Story of Drumchapel. Glasgow Drumchapel Heritage Group.

288 Crotty, J.G. (2004). Your place or mine? Issues of power, participation and partnership in an urban regeneration area. University of Glasgow.

289 Calder, J. & Johnston, G. (1989). Drumchapel The Frustration Game. [online] Available: https://www.youtube.com/watch?v=cvwKjd7OD20 [Accessed 7 June 2021].

290 Glasgow City Council (2022). Works Delivered to Reduce Flood Risk in Drumchapel. [online] Available at: https://www.glasgow.gov.uk/index.aspx?articleid=29053 [Accessed 3 March 2022].

291 Glasgow City Council (2018). Kelvingrove Park Conservation Area Appraisal. Glasgow City Council.

292 Yorkhill & Kelvingrove Development Trust (2022). Yorkhill and Kelvingrove Cycling Village Summary.

Acknowledgments

In times of turmoil and danger, gratitude helps to steady and
ground us. It brings us into presence, and our full presence is
perhaps the best offering we can make to our world.
~ Joanna Macy ~

I am grateful for the unwavering and rigorous mentoring of my
supervisors Dr Anne Cumming and Dr Husam Al Waer, who
accompanied me during rewarding breakthroughs, moments of
frustration, stagnant periods and times of inspiration
throughout my PhD journey. I also extend my gratitude to a
wider circle of academics within the Architecture and Urban
Planning school at the University of Dundee, especially Dr
Dumiso Moyo, for opening the door of academia to practitioners
and for encouraging me to pursue my doctorate. I must also
express my heartfelt appreciation to Pamela Mang from
Regenesis Institute, who nurtured an instigating mentor-
mentee relationship and for her profound vision of regenerative
pathways for humanity and the planet which serves as a great
inspiration for this work.

Deep gratitude to Edinburgh City Council, Glasgow City Council
and Perth & Kinross City Council senior planners and officials,
who believed in the relevance of my research and introduced
me to the neighbourhood's 'gatekeepers', so paving the way for
bountiful participant recruitment. I would also like to express
my sincere gratitude to my research participants. Without the
generosity of the 274 women who joined the walking interviews
and shared their time, this book would have not materialised. I
have been profoundly enriched by the depth of their thinking
and their insightful contributions.

I need to acknowledge two irreplaceable colleagues from the
Highlands of Scotland: Cathel de Lima Hutchison in his role as

tireless proof-reader and challenger of assumptions, and Sebastian Franke for turning mental sketches into clear cut diagrams and designs.

My sincere thanks also go to Daniel Wahl who introduced me to Andrew Carey from Triarchy Press, who in turn gave me a vote of confidence in publishing this book. My very special thanks go to my editor, Debbie Frances, who breathed vitality into the manuscript, transmuted unnecessary jargon and marshalled this book towards the bookshelves.

My loving gratitude to my daughters, Inanna and Tara, and my sister, Christina, for their continuing reassurance and for 'holding the space' during my long writing retreats. Thanks also to my continental, transatlantic and friends from 'The Shore' in Leith as sources of encouragement, contentiousness and amusement.

Finally, I am indebted to a lineage of women who complemented radical critiques of urbanism with new frameworks and practices for enhancing women's everyday urban experiences. Amongst them the contributions of Catherine Bauer (1934), Jane Jacobs (1961), Dolores Hayden (1981), Elizabeth Wilson (1991), Leslie Kanes Weisman (1992), Daphne Spain (1992), Doreen Massey (1994), Diana Agrest (1996), Dory Reeves (2004), Hilde Heynen (2005), Doina Petrescu (2007), Laura Elkin (2017), and Leslie Kern (2021) stand strong and enduring, and without whose engagement with these issues I could not have begun my own journey to do so.

About the Author

May East was born in São Paulo and now lives in Edinburgh. She is an international urbanist and regenerative practitioner bringing vitality and viability to eco-communities, mining cities, indigenous villages, informal settlements, transition and ghost towns. She currently works with local & regional government, private sector and intergovernmental agencies providing policy guidance for initiatives aimed at enhancing gender-sensitive urban planning, decreasing carbon emissions, establishing sovereign wealth funds, and developing symbiotic eco-industrial parks.

May's career portfolio spans diverse disciplines and areas of interest. She comes from a thriving artistic community between São Paulo and Rio de Janeiro where for over a decade, her art, be it in music, film or video, expressed a deep concern for all of Brazil's diverse environments, both in the major cities and the country's vast interior, especially the Amazonian rainforests.

Associated with UNITAR for two decades, May currently serves as Advisory Member of the Division for People and Social Inclusion. She is a specialist in promoting vertical integration between community-led solutions to climate resilience and national & international donors, and the UN system and conventions. She holds a Master of Science in Spatial Planning with specialisation in the rehabilitation of abandoned villages and towns, and a PhD in Architecture and Urban Planning with the University of Dundee on the topic What if Women Designed the City?.

May was designated as one of the 100 Global SustainAbility Leaders three years in a row and Women of the Decade in Sustainability and Leadership by Women Economic Forum.

About Triarchy Press

Triarchy Press is an independent publisher of books that bring a systemic or contextual approach to many areas of life, including:

Government, Education, Health and other public services ~ Ecology and Regenerative Cultures ~ Leading and Managing Organisations ~ The Money System ~ Psychotherapy and other Expressive Therapies ~ Walking, Psychogeography and Mythogeography ~ Movement and Somatics ~ Innovation ~ The Future and Future Studies

Other related titles by Triarchy Press include:

* Designing Regenerative Cultures ~ **Daniel Christian Wahl**
* Combining ~ **Nora Bateson**
* Flourish ~ **Sarah Ichioka & Michael Pawlyn**
* The Architect Walker ~ **Wrights & Sites**
* Terminalian Drift – **Jerry Gordon**

For more details, and to purchase any of these titles, visit:

www.triarchypress.net